BY RICHAR
WITH PORTRA
SAMUE

If I could tell you just <u>one</u> thing...

ENCOUNTERS WITH
REMARKABLE PEOPLE
AND THEIR MOST
VALUABLE ADVICE

CANONGATE

Edinburgh · London

Published in Great Britain in 2016 by
Canongate Books Ltd, 14 High Street, Edinburgh EH1 1TE

www.canongate.co.uk

5

British Library Cataloguing-in-Publication Data
A catalogue record for this book is available on
request from the British Library

ISBN 978 1 78211 922 7

Typeset in Bembo by Palimpsest Book Production Ltd,
Falkirk, Stirlingshire

Printed and bound in Great Britain by Clays Ltd, St Ives plc.

To Chicken and Sausage

CONTENTS

INTRODUCTION

WHEN I WAS A CHILD my father often took me fell walking. We spent misty days climbing the gentle peaks of the Yorkshire Dales and Lakeland crags. Each trip a new route, a different summit to climb, always a bar of chocolate at the top.

I don't remember him teaching me per se, but I inherited from him the rituals of the Great Outdoors: close the gate to keep the sheep in, walk at the edge of the field to protect the crops, stand aside for those coming uphill.

My favourite tradition was placing a stone on the cairns, the small pile of rocks that walkers create to help mark the way. A simple, easy practice, both altruistic and self-preserving in its aim: to help others find their path, knowing that the next time the lost fell walker could be you.

We benefited from those cairns ourselves many times, when the clouds came in and the path was unclear. And even on bright days, those cairns provided welcome reassurance, while more distant ones hinted at different paths still to explore.

Off the mountains, I've come to appreciate that sometimes a few words of advice can act as cairn stones in life; a wise sentence or two that get you back on course when you're lost in the fog or stuck in boggy terrain, knowledge from a fellow traveller who can point out the best views of the safest route.

On at least three occasions a single piece of advice has changed my life. And over the years I've gained a deep appreciation of learning from people both wiser and more experienced than myself. So ten years ago I made a simple promise to myself: whenever I met someone remarkable, I'd ask them for their best piece of advice.

The result is this book.

If I Could Tell You Just One Thing . . . walks the full spectrum of human experiences and emotions, from those of Simon Cowell at one end to those of Lily Ebert, an Auschwitz survivor, at the other. In between, you'll find the considered wisdom of presidents and popstars, entrepreneurs and artists, celebrities and survivors; from people who've made it and from others who have endured incredible hardships, from those who've climbed as high as you can go in life, and from people who've witnessed the worst of what humans can do to one another.

Good advice is like a nutrient-rich broth, made from boiling down the bones of life. And being fed so much of it, sourced from such remarkable people, has enriched my life and understanding of my fellow homosapiens immeasurably. If chosen well, a few words can capture and disseminate the main insights gained from someone's hard years of experience, thereby allowing us all to benefit from them. That is certainly the aim of each of the encounters in the book.

Every person is someone I've met, either through running my

own business, or from my subsequent varied career working in government, charities, the arts and the media. Some people featured are friends, some are people who generously agreed to be interviewed, and a few are unsuspecting folk I ambushed when fate put us in the same room at a party, a conference or, in one case, at a urinal.

When I ask people for their best piece of advice, I urge them to really think about what they consider to be *most* important. I put the exact same question to everyone: *Given all that you have experienced, given all that you now know and given all that you have learnt, if you could pass on only one piece of advice, what would it be?* There is something about asking people to stand behind just one nugget of wisdom that gets them to reflect harder, dig deeper and be more candid in their response. And it has led to some extraordinary answers. The material is diverse and wide ranging, and covers everything from achieving success to dealing with failure, from finding love to having better sex, from getting the best out of people to surviving abuse. There should be something in this collection that speaks to everyone.

Most people when asked for advice are happy to give it. This desire to help is a manifestation of the better part of human nature; it costs nothing, can be shared infinitely and will last indefinitely. And I hope that this is the first of several books. For there are countless remarkable people on the planet, and this first collection only captures the insights of a fraction of them. There are endless stories to be told and wisdom to be captured.

Over time I hope to help create a global commons of advice, a shared pool of wisdom that everyone can both contribute to and gain from. After all, as a species we are much more alike than we are different. And while everyone's path through life is unique, we can all benefit from the knowledge of more experienced walkers ahead, who can tell us of the most beautiful things to see and guide us to the safer places to cross the river.

Richard Reed

June 2016

IN THE BUBBLE WITH
PRESIDENT CLINTON

HIS STAFFERS CALL IT BEING in 'The Bubble', the experience of travelling in President Clinton's entourage. You ride in the President's plane, drive in his armed convoy, sit at his table. You don't so much as move, you *glide*. There's no queuing for passport control, no checking in, no checking out – it all just happens behind the scenes. You go wherever and whenever Mr President goes.

I got to ride in The Bubble on a Clinton Foundation trip round Africa. It was a gruelling schedule: eight African countries in eight days. Every day the same: wake up in a new country, get in the convoy, drive hours down dusty tracks and potholed paths into the middle of nowhere, visit a project – an HIV testing clinic, a malaria treatment facility, a woman's empowerment group – then back in the jeeps and on to the next project, at least four times a day.

At each visit, the President was an unstoppable force: straight out of the 4x4, hug the local community nurses, talk with the dignitaries, dance with the local tribal performers, pose for the photos, do the speech, present the gong, stop and chat with the locals, play with the kids, notice the quiet one at the back, make a point of talking to them, give them a hug, coax out that smile. At every event. In the searing heat and dust, all day, for eight days straight. I've not seen anything like it. I don't think anyone has.

He reflected for a while when I asked my question about advice for life in a rare moment between stops. But the President's answer made sense of what we were seeing:

> *'I've come to believe that one of the most important things is to see people. The person who opens the door for you, the person who pours your coffee. Acknowledge them. Show them respect. The traditional greeting of the Zulu people of South Africa is "Sawubona". It means "I see you". I try and do that.'*

Never has a person practised more what they preach.

The craziest bit, back at the hotel, after twelve hours in the field, tired, dusty, depleted, when us mere mortals would be up in our rooms ordering room service and hiding, President Clinton is down in the dining room talking to the waiters, joking with the other guests, making an American couple's honeymoon, accepting an invitation to join a family's table, sitting with Mum, Dad and two saucer-eyed children. He doesn't stop. He knows what it means to people to meet a President, or more specifically to meet *him*. And *everyone* is made welcome. Everyone is made to feel important. Everyone is *seen*.

'ONE OF THE MOST IMPORTANT
THINGS IS TO SEE PEOPLE.
THE PERSON WHO OPENS
THE DOOR FOR YOU, THE
PERSON WHO POURS YOUR
COFFEE. ACKNOWLEDGE THEM.
SHOW THEM RESPECT.'

– *Bill Clinton*

MARINA ABRAMOVIĆ
IS PRESENT

I'M IN DOWNTOWN NEW YORK looking for soup. Specifically chicken noodle soup *with* prawns, or, I am now wondering, did she say *without* prawns? I arranged this lunchtime meeting with Marina Abramović, the Serbian-born, internationally revered performance artist, a month ago and we agreed I would bring her favourite soup. I just can't remember what it is.

To avoid a potential faux pas, I get both. So when I arrive in the Greenwich studio where Marina works, the first order of business is to decide who gets which soup. Personal preferences are to be discarded; she insists on tossing a coin. Fate shall decide.

The fact that I worried she may be upset about which soup she gets both shows my hopeless Britishness and ignores the fact that this is an artist who has flagellated, cut and burnt her naked body for her art in public on many occasions. She is probably not the type to get worried about soup.

In fact, she is a woman who fits no type at all. She is gloriously, gorgeously unique and manages simultaneously to be sincere, saucy (she likes telling dirty Serbian jokes*), free-living, disciplined, reckless and loving, and is about the most interesting and alive human being I have ever met.

In her performance art over the years she has pushed herself to the point where she has lost consciousness, gained scars, spilt blood and risked her life. One of her earlier works, *Rhythm 0*, involved her lying on a table while people were given access to seventy-two different objects – scissors, a feather, a scalpel, honey, a whip, etc. – and told to use them on her as they saw fit. By the end she'd been stripped naked, had her neck cut, thorns pressed into her stomach and a gun put to her head.

She has recently hit seventy and is more in demand than ever before. MOMA's 2010 retrospective of her work, 'The Artist Is Present', super-charged her international profile. As part of this exhibition, she sat immobile and silent in a chair for over seven hundred hours while thousands of visitors queued, some overnight, to sit opposite her. Marina would hold eye contact with each person, fully present in the moment, reacting to them only if they cried, by her crying too.

She explains that being present, gaining consciousness, is a big theme in her work. She sees cultivating inner-awareness as the best way to disentangle ourselves from the artificial structures of society, so we don't feel disempowered or helpless. *'With many people, there is a sense the world is falling apart and it creates a feeling of just giving up. And that inertia is the real danger to society.*

MARINA ABRAMOVIĆ

❖

6

___

*'How do Montenegro men masturbate? They put it in the earth and wait for an earthquake' (Apparently a favourite Serbian joke about how lazy Montenegrin men are. With apologies to all our male Montenegrin readers. Source: Abramović, M.).

People have to realise we can create change by changing ourselves.'

This heightened consciousness can only come if we stop thinking and achieve a state of mental emptiness; only then can we receive what Marina calls *'liquid knowledge – the knowledge that is universal and belongs to everyone'*. The mission to help people attain it explains her more recent work, in which she invites her audience to count grains of rice or water droplets, to open the same door over and over again, to *'create distractions to stop distraction, and rediscover the present so they can then rediscover themselves'*.

Given the originality and uncompromising nature of her work, the risks she has taken and the sacrifices she has made, it is unsurprising that her main piece of advice is a rallying cry to commit deeply to whatever it is you feel that you must do.

> **'Today 100 per cent is not enough. Give 100 per cent, and then go over this border into what is more than you can do. You have to take the unknown journey to where nobody has ever been, because that is how civilisation moves forwards. 100 per cent is not enough. 150 per cent is just good enough.'**

I hugely respect the advice, but I reply that most people may not be prepared to put themselves in harm's way and in real pain for their passions as she has done. But for this too she has advice. *'Yes, the pain can be terrible,'* she replies, *'but if you say to yourself "So what? So Pain, what can you do?" and if you accept pain and are no longer afraid of it, you will cross the gate into the non-pain state.'*

Advice I choose to accept rather than put to the test.

MARINA ABRAMOVIĆ

❖

7

'Today 100 per cent is not enough. Give 100 per cent, and then go over this border into what is more than you can do. You have to take the unknown journey to

WHERE NOBODY HAS EVER
BEEN, BECAUSE THAT IS
HOW CIVILISATION MOVES
FORWARDS. 100 PER CENT IS
NOT ENOUGH. 150 PER CENT IS
JUST GOOD ENOUGH.'

— *Marina Abramović*

TERRY WAITE, A PATIENT MAN

I'VE JUST HEARD WHAT MUST be one of the most understated sentences a human being could utter. I'm having lunch with Terry Waite in his local cathedral town of Bury St Edmunds. He is telling me about his experience of being held hostage for five years in Lebanon in the late 1980s, after having gone there as the Church of England's envoy to negotiate the release of existing prisoners. He describes his four years of solitary confinement in a tiny, windowless cell, chained to a wall. He recounts the beatings and mock executions he suffered. He explains how he had to put on a blindfold if a guard came into the cell, so he didn't see a human face for four years, and how they refused him a pen, paper and books and any communication with the outside world, including his family. He reflects back on it all and says, *'Yes, it was a bit isolating.'*

Terry Waite is the human manifestation of what it means to be humble, to serve and to sacrifice. He put himself in harm's way in the hope that he could help others. And twenty-five years later he is still working tirelessly to help people who have had family members taken hostage, which says it all.

The craziest thing is that he claims he was mainly doing it for himself. I tell him I know the concept that no charitable gesture is selfless, but this is pushing it. He insists, saying his career has been about achieving reconciliations and that following that path has helped him reconcile the different sides of his own self.

He is also quick to point out that many people have to endure far more than he did. He talks of people held captive in their own body, when disease or accident have taken away their ability to move. And he knows only too well of the many hostages who don't get to come home at all.

Both Terry's words and actions advocate the profound importance of having empathy: it is a fundamental tenet of his approach to life. He recounts meeting with the British mother of a man who was beheaded by terrorists in Iraq, who even in her terrible grief said that she knew her suffering was no different to that of a mother in Iraq who has lost her son through warfare or insurgency. *'In that simple statement she summed up with tremendous courage something we should never forget: we are all members of the same human family. We all have fears, and hopes and aspirations. We all have our vulnerabilities, so we should be very careful before we attribute negative stereotypes to other people.'*

Terry's empathy helped him stick to the three rules he set himself when he realised that he'd been taken hostage: no regrets, no self-pity and no sentimentality. He also stuck to his principle of non-violence, a philosophy tested to the extreme when one day he found a gun in the toilet left accidentally by his guard. (Terry said *'I think you've forgotten something'* and handed it back to him.)

So, how does one cope with four years of entirely unjust and unrelenting solitary confinement?

'I did my best to structure each day. I would allocate a period of time to doing my exercises, then I would write for an hour or two in my head, then do mental arithmetic. And I spent a lot of time dreaming up poetry too. And then it would be time for some more exercises. And so on.'

I tell him it seems it would be impossibly hard to fill all those lonely hours. In another world-class example of being understated, Terry just nods and responds, *'You know, the whole experience wouldn't have been so bad if they'd just let me have some books.'*

He claims there have been unintended benefits of the ordeal. It gave him the confidence to leave his salaried job afterwards and live a freer life. So one related piece of wisdom he is keen to pass on is that every disaster, or seeming disaster, in life can usually be turned around and something creative can emerge from it. *'That is not to say such suffering is not difficult and damn hard, but it doesn't need be totally destructive. It's the way you approach it, and the way you approach life after.'*

So, given that, what is his best advice for how to approach life?

'It's the same lesson I learnt in that cell. What you have to do is live for the day, you have to say, now is life, this very moment. It's not tomorrow, it's not yesterday, it's now, so you have to live it as fully as you can. Invest in every day.'

After speaking to Terry, I will.

❖

ABSOLUTELY LUMLEY

I'M AT AN AWARDS DO and the god of seating plans has smiled benevolently upon me. I'm sat next to Joanna Lumley, one of the UK's most loved actresses, and also one of the country's most prolific and effective activists. To talk to, she is as one would expect. Warm, inclusive, crush-inducing. But with these soft-edged charms come inspiring, hard-edged principles: a sense of civic duty, of justice, of doing the right thing. She is a heady combination of warm heart and iron will. Which explains that while her TV and film work would be a career to be proud of in itself, it is her commitments and contributions off screen that are the most remarkable.

Take the new Garden Bridge across the Thames in London. An idea soon to become reality, providing the most beautiful addition to the city this century. Everyone in London knows about it and everybody loves it. Just like Joanna Lumley. But what is less known is that it was entirely her idea, a concept she dreamt up and then agitated to make happen, bending the will of those who naively told her at first it couldn't be done.

Or look at the issue of Nepalese Gurkha veterans (who served in the British armed forces before 1997), who have been historically denied the right to settle in the UK after fighting *for* the country – a morally bankrupt decision and one that needed reversing. It was an unfashionable and unfabulous fight, but one that Joanna Lumley took on unreservedly, using her charm, celebrity, conviction and sheer dogged resilience until the victory was achieved and those rights installed.

In short, she is no ordinary woman.

And when I give a short speech later at the awards do and say I've been sitting next to Joanna Lumley, the audience erupt into applause: everyone in the room loves her.

There was therefore a synchronicity to the advice she gave me.

> *'The secret, darling, is to love everyone you meet. From the moment you meet them. Give everyone the benefit of the doubt. Start from a position that they are lovely and that you will love them. Most people will respond to that and be lovely and love you back and it becomes a self-fulfilling prophecy, and you can then achieve the most wonderful things.'*

Then she leant forward and whispered in my ear.

> *'But get rid of any of the bastards that let you down.'*

As I said: warm heart, iron will.

'THE SECRET, DARLING,
IS TO LOVE EVERYONE YOU
MEET. FROM THE MOMENT
YOU MEET THEM. GIVE
EVERYONE THE BENEFIT
OF THE DOUBT.'

— *Joanna Lumley*

THE ELOQUENT MR FRY

THE PREVIOUS TIME I SPOKE with Stephen Fry he was a robot. The setting was a tech conference, and he attended via an iPad attached to a cyborg-on-wheels, controlled remotely from a joystick and camera in his bedroom. This time, we're chatting in person over afternoon tea, sipping from bone china cups in a cosy members' club in London. The different interactions capture two sides of a fascinating man: on the one hand, a self-confessed techno-geek with an interest in the latest gadgets, and on the other a graceful British gentleman with a love of classic traditions and culture.

As you would imagine, meeting his real, rather than virtual, self is the richer of the two encounters. In person you experience his warmth and thoughtfulness, and a wonderful sense of complicity from the stories and confessions he weaves into the conversation. He's an easy man to spend time with.

Modestly, he says advice is something he is wary of giving, but he does have a few thoughts he'd be happy to share. I am expecting something literary or spiritual, but surprisingly his first thought is a broadsiding of life-coaching. *'One piece of advice I want to give is avoid all life-coach lessons; they are snake oil, without exception, and the art of stating the so-fucking-obvious it makes your nose bleed.'*

I was not, it has to be said, expecting *that*.

When I query why, he expands further. One reason is '*their obsession with goal-setting. Because if I meet my goals, what then? Is that it, is my life over? I met my goal, do I just set another one? What's the meaning of the first goal if the second one has to be set? Or if I don't meet it, am I a failure?'*

As he talks, I subtly turn over the page in the notebook that lists my goals for the day.

Unsurprisingly, Stephen does not have a life coach. But he does have Noël Coward. And a quotation from him, which Stephen has above his desk, guides his approach to life: Work is more fun than fun.

'*If you can make that true of your work, you will have a wonderful life. I know how lucky I am to have found that, and how unlucky so many are to have not found that. People talk about work–life balance. But the idea of balancing one against the other makes no sense. My work isn't against my life – work is my life.'*

Of course, just loving your work is not enough; if you want to get anywhere, you have to be prepared to work really hard at it too. '*Everyone I know who is successful works, and works hard. Really hard. Maybe that should be my advice: work your bloody bollocks off.'*

But the strongest recommendation Stephen has is to avoid the trap of thinking it is somehow easier for other people.

'It is never right to look at someone successful and think "That person's got money, that person's got looks, that

❖ STEPHEN FRY

20

person's good at cricket . . . so it's easier for them." Chances are, 90 per cent of the time you're wrong. But even if it is somehow true, thinking that is a very self-destructive thing. It leads only to resentment, which is corrosive and destroys everything but itself.'

Stephen believes it is better to try and put yourself in their shoes. Imagine what life is like for them.

'It is the secret of art, and it is the secret of life: the more time you spend imagining what it's like to be someone else, the more you develop empathy for others, the easier it is to know yourself and to be yourself.'

Which is the best thing for us all to be.

'Work your bloody

bollocks off.'

– STEPHEN FRY

THE EROTIC INTELLIGENCE OF
ESTHER PEREL

T HIS IS PERHAPS THE ULTIMATE sign of the times: I am
at an international tech conference, featuring literally
thousands of founders of cutting-edge internet companies, but the talk *everyone* wants to hear is Esther Perel's, the
world's most renowned relationship therapist and advisor-in-chief
on handling intimacy in the modern age.

Esther is ready to speak, but the organisers won't let her. We're
in the main auditorium and there are 500 more people than there
are seats. Founders are sat on the steps, stood at the back, crammed
into the doorways. However, the fire regulations won't allow for
such numbers, so an announcement is made: until the extra 500
people leave, Esther can't start. But no one is prepared to miss
out and a stand-off ensues. It's resolved only by Esther promising
to repeat the talk later for the people who can't stay. In fact, such
is the demand that over the weekend she ends up giving four
talks. In comparison, the founder of Uber gives just one.

I catch up with Esther later, in her current hometown of New
York. I ask her why she thinks so many people were keen to get
her advice on sex and relationships. She explains, *'We have gone,*

at this point, into a digitalised way of life, a generation that has been clicking away forever, in environments that are sensorially deprived. And it creates a corrective need, for human contact, for face-to-face relationships, but after the digital world we can often struggle with the imperfect nature of real people.'

The fact that people immersed in the online world sometimes need help with handling real life is not something she judges or condemns, but it is something she occasionally worries about. *'There can be something beautiful about the immediacy of connection that the digital world allows, but on the other hand dating apps where we swipe left or right can leave people feeling disposable, commodified even, and that commodification is hurtful and degrading.'*

Esther first received international acclaim for her insights into relationships when she published her book *Mating in Captivity*, an exploration of 'erotic intelligence' and how to keep sex alive in long-term relationships. Esther brought into the open the underlying contradictions in coupling-up: the fact that we crave both freedom and security, the predictability love needs yet the novelty desire longs for. It gave some straight-talking solutions and has been credited with saving countless relationships ever since.

Beyond the actual content of her work, the most fascinating thing is why Esther was drawn to studying people and relationships in the first place. *'My interest in people, in humanity, in the way people live, whether they create a life of meaning or not, it goes back to my two parents, who are Holocaust survivors. They both spent four years plus in concentration camps and came out with nothing. All they had was themselves, their sense of decency and their relationship. That is what endured. And my dad said that was all that mattered.'*

And her father's wisdom echoes in the advice Esther gives, which is among the best and most profound I've heard:

> *'The quality of your life ultimately depends on the quality of your relationships. Not on your achievements, not on how smart you are, not on how rich you are, but on the quality of your relationships, which are basically a reflection of your sense of decency, your ability to think of others, your generosity. Ultimately at the end of your life, if people commend you, they will say what a wonderful human being you were, and when they talk about the human being that you were, it won't be the fact that you had a big bank account, it really won't. It will be about how you treated the people around you and how you made them feel.'*

'The quality of your life ultimately depends on the quality of your relationships. Not on your achievements, not on how smart you are, not on how rich you are,

BUT ON THE QUALITY OF YOUR
RELATIONSHIPS, WHICH ARE
BASICALLY A REFLECTION
OF YOUR SENSE OF DECENCY,
YOUR ABILITY TO THINK OF
OTHERS, YOUR GENEROSITY.'

– *Esther Perel*

INSIDE HESTON BLUMENTHAL

I T'S NOT GOING WELL. THE score is 10–1, match-point to Heston Blumenthal. The Michelin three-starred chef and owner of the best restaurant in the world (as voted for by the best chefs in the world) turns out to also be a fiend at table tennis. In my defence, before the match started he plied me with strange-coloured cocktails and confessed to having table-tennis lessons up to three times a week. At least the humiliation is swift: his final serve goes the way we both know it's going to, and I retire to the bench and to the solace of my next cocktail.

The experience of going to see Heston at home is the British middle-class equivalent of visiting Hunter S. Thompson: liquor is drunk, cigars are smoked, deep chats are had, and while no guns get fired, he does have his table-tennis serving machine, a device that shoots out one hundred balls a minute. We turn it on and it causes a hailstorm of the little blighters pinging off every wall and surface in his table tennis-dedicated basement.

I've known Heston for a while now. His brain is like that ping-pong machine, capable of throwing out a hundred ideas a minute. His curiosity, creativity and appetite for learning are greater than in anyone I know. The first time we met was at a company meeting, where I watched him get 300 people to each eat an apple holding their noses, to demonstrate how flavour is what we smell, not what we taste. He is a man who lives and, literally, breathes sensory experiences. And to illustrate the point, we're now back in his kitchen and he's teaching me how to smoke a cigar so you can appreciate all the different flavours. It involves repeatedly pulling a lit cigar from his lips with a pronounced 'schmack' sound; the trick apparently is to *'keep the smoke out of your mouth, don't let it get past your teeth'*.

Food doesn't just play a central role in Heston's life, he sees it as a way of explaining all of human existence; food has shaped not just what we do and who we are, but also *what* we are.

'We evolved because of eating and the things around eating . . . when we discovered fire we moved away from eating only raw starches, our lower digestion started to shrink, our neck and therefore our larynx lengthened, which allowed us over time to start to vocalise. And that ability to communicate meant we could start to spread ideas, build up our imaginations and from that everything became possible.'

Connecting food to human imagination is his signature dish. He's brought more original ideas into the kitchen than anyone else. He first got major attention in the culinary world when his restaurant, The Fat Duck, put crab ice cream on the menu – a dish that now seems almost ordinary in the food fantasy world he's since created of edible pubs, food you can listen to and chocolates that float in mid-air.

He says his interest in the world of food went from zero to one hundred in a lunchtime: as a teenager, his dad got a bonus from work and to celebrate he took the family to a Michelin three-starred restaurant in France. The combination of not just the food and the tastes but the sensory overload of the smell of lavender from the restaurant garden, the feel of linen on the table, the crunch of gravel underfoot, the sounds of crickets and clinking glasses: *'It felt like I'd gone down this rabbit hole into wonderland and I found something that fascinated me and I knew right then I wanted to be a chef.'*

His imagination and curiosity were kick-started by studying ice cream. He found a recipe from 1870 for Parmesan ice cream. *'I thought, "That's bizarre!" and then I started questioning why was it bizarre, who says ice cream has to be sweet? And once I started questioning that, I began questioning everything. I found that thread and just kept on pulling.'*

It means that while your average chef is checking out other restaurants and menus for inspiration, Heston will be investigating the worlds of biology, chemistry, history and geography. He has teamed up with professors in macrobiotics, psychologists and molecular scientists. As an example of how deep he can go in these lines of enquiry, this year the Royal Society of Chemists is publishing a list of 175 of the most influential scientists and chemists on the planet, alive or dead. Einstein's on it, so is Heston.

He leads me over to a coat of arms he created, now framed on the kitchen wall. He says it took him seven years to design, as he wanted to capture everything he stood for. There is a twig of lavender to reflect smell and the trip to that first restaurant, a pair of hands to reflect the craft of his work, a Tudor Rose for the historical element of his cooking, a magnifying glass for the importance of investigation and enquiry, and an apple to reflect

Newton's discovery and non-linear thinking. Most telling of all is his motto, just two words, inscribed in italic font, which explain his approach and his creativity and what he puts forward as his best piece of advice for life:

'Question everything.'

And to me he expands:

'The opposite of question everything is question nothing. And if you don't question things, there's no knowledge, no learning, no creativity, no freedom of choice, no imagination. So I always ask why. And why not. I ask question, question, question, question. And then I listen. And that's how I discover something new.'

He then concludes by asking me a question. It's the one I am most dreading: *'Fancy another game of table tennis?'*

'QUESTION EVERYTHING . . .
IF YOU DON'T QUESTION THINGS,
THERE'S NO KNOWLEDGE, NO
LEARNING, NO CREATIVITY,
NO FREEDOM OF CHOICE, NO
IMAGINATION.'

– *Heston Blumenthal*

THE TWO VOICES
OF ANNIE LENNOX

ANNIE LENNOX HAS TWO VOICES. The first is the one that has sold over eighty million albums, winning her five Grammys, an Academy Award and more Brit Awards than any other female artist. Her second voice is the one she lends to women's rights and the issue of HIV/AIDS in Africa. And it's this campaigning voice that takes centre stage these days.

Annie remembers the moment when her singing voice changed pitch from artistry to activism. It was after taking part in a concert to launch 46664, Nelson Mandela's HIV/AIDS foundation in South Africa, a country with the highest rate of HIV infection in the world. She witnessed Mandela describe the HIV pandemic as *'a silent genocide, carrying the face of women'*. He explained that one in three pregnant women were HIV positive in South Africa and AIDS was (and still is) a leading cause of death for women of reproductive age globally. Then, on a visit to a township hospital, she saw the impact of AIDS for herself, in clinics, rape crisis centres, orphanages and people's homes. It was a dark epiphany for Annie. From then on, she shaped her life around responding to the tragedy.

The result has been over a decade of tireless work on tackling the issue – work that has, according to Archbishop Desmond Tutu, '*contributed significantly to turning the pandemic around in our country*'. In 2007 she founded a campaign called SING to raise global awareness and prompt action, helping to ensure that HIV positive women and children have access to the treatment and care they need. Annie has travelled across the globe giving fund-raising performances, presentations, speeches and interviews on radio, television and in the printed press, at conferences, rallies and in government buildings, speaking truth to power at every given opportunity. She also became the founder of The Circle, an organisation which aims to inspire and connect women in order to harness their skills, creativity and influence, and to transform the challenges and injustices faced by the most disempowered girls and women in the world.

Those dusty plains of Sub-Saharan Africa are a long way from the working-class tenement block in Aberdeen where she was raised. Coming from a poor but musical family, she studied the piano and flute at school, which led her to be offered a place at the Royal Academy of Music in London at the age of seventeen. '*It became my passport out of there.*'

Tough years followed, however. '*I had very little money and didn't really know anyone. I lived in a variety of different bedsits, doing whatever I could to make ends meet, but even though my chances seemed bleak I didn't want to go back to Scotland and feel as if I'd failed.*'

One constant through it all was singing. '*I would sing and sing and sing, walking down the street, in the shower, all the time, just by myself, and by the time three years at the Royal Academy had come to*

ANNIE LENNOX

❖

38

an end I knew I wanted to be a singer/songwriter, so I started to write songs on an old Victorian harmonium. I'd been writing poems since I was twelve and I had a lot to say.'

But for all the hard work, practice and passion, one factor for success was still missing: serendipity. That came thanks to Camden Market, where Annie sold second-hand clothes, sharing a stall with a friend. It was there that she got to know a guy selling records who told her, *'You should meet my mate, Dave.'* According to Annie there was a creative connection with Dave Stewart from the beginning and within a few years they were dominating the charts on both sides of the Atlantic as Eurythmics.

Her life story is of a woman following her passions, wherever they may take her, from the tenements of Aberdeen to the townships of Africa, via the Grammys in America, and her advice fits that story perfectly.

'There will be "Ah ha!" moments in life when a light might go on, when you think to yourself, "I MUST do that" – whatever it is. It's not because someone says you should do it, but it's because you feel absolutely compelled to and there would be something wrong with the world if you didn't. If you find that light – acknowledge it. Find other people who share that passion. Cultivate it. Find that deeper purpose in your life.'

As voices go, it's a good one to listen to.

ON HOLIDAY
WITH SIMON COWELL

I'M SAT DEEP IN THE stalls of the London Palladium theatre, watching four glamorously dressed people on stage argue with each other. Above them hangs a huge backlit Union Jack resplendent with the words 'Britain's Got Talent'. And beneath it sits the man who has most definitively proved that assertion to be true: Simon Cowell.

After the judges finish play-fighting and filming wraps for the day, I'm brought backstage to meet the main man. He's sat in the centre of the room, surrounded by a bustle of black-clad assistants, cameramen and producers: the calm eye in the middle of his own media storm.

I know his reputation for cutting to the chase, to put it politely. I also know from his media director that he's twelve hours into a twenty-hour day, so I am a little apprehensive, expecting a terse, short conversation. But the exact opposite ensues and, embarrassingly for a forty-three-year-old straight man such as myself, over the hour we spend talking I fall hopelessly and completely in love with Simon Cowell.

It starts with Simon sitting me down and making sure I am

comfortable. He then offers me a cup of his homemade fresh ginger tea, but it turns out to be so fiery I start to cough and my eyes water uncontrollably. Simon is concerned and makes sure I am OK. Then, once he is happy I've recovered, spends the next ten minutes enquiring about me, my business, my story. He speaks softly, probes gently, listens intently. He invests more time just asking about me than the time we've been allocated to talk.

Eventually he allows me to move the topic of the conversation from me to him. His manner is so warm and kind and charming, and his voice so soothing, I totally relax. A lovely feeling washes over me, like being on a sunny holiday. He uses my name a lot and drops in the odd compliment. I get the impression he really likes me. I start to think we might become good friends. Maybe we'll even go on holiday together.

I catch myself. This is ridiculous. I'm a grown man behaving like a teenager. I need to concentrate. I push my man crush and daydreams to one side and tune back in to what he's saying. He's certainly someone worth listening to: a rich and fertile source of practical wisdom and insight, anecdotes and stories. I say his team strike me as exceptional in their commitment and professionalism, and he explains how he learnt to get the best from people. *'Well, Richard, my dad told me there's an invisible sign on everyone's head which says make me feel important. Remember that and you'll be fine.'*

He's charmingly, self-deprecatingly candid about where his ideas come from, which makes me like him even more. *'So, Richard, I'm in my kitchen one night, cooking dinner and watching some boring programme, saying to myself, "I'd rather watch a dancing dog than this,"* and then a few seconds later I think, *"Actually, I really would rather be watching a dancing dog than this."* And that's where the idea for BGT came from.'

I can see his assistants hovering, but I don't want my time in the sun to end, so I play for time and keep on asking questions. Given his dominance in the music industry, what's his advice for aspiring artists trying to make it? *'More than anything else, you've got to have a great song. Do small gigs. Listen to the crowd's reaction, find out what works.'* And how does one cope with all the inevitable rejections? *'Listen to the feedback, you may learn from it. But if the people saying "No" are more stupid than you, don't get discouraged.'* What if someone finds themself auditioning or pitching to Simon Cowell? *'If you get a "Yes", then shut up. There are times I've said yes and the artist starts with "I knew it, we're going to do amazing things together" and the more they talk the more I'm thinking, "I'm really going off you". The better ones just say "Good, call my lawyer" and leave. That confidence has me reaching for my lawyer within ten seconds.'*

I would keep going all night if I could, but I know that sadly all holidays come to an end. And with local versions of his shows running in more than 180 countries, Simon has a long night ahead of him, with many questions to be answered, many auditions to watch, many people to make feel important.

So I finish by asking for his number-one piece of advice.

'My best advice is listen, listen rather than talk. I was never bright in school, but I was a very good listener, and I still am. I have a better life because of it. When I meet

people, I'm curious about their story, about how they did what they did. Along the way you meet people smarter than you and they teach you what you don't already know. So I listen to them, take away my little titbits, and off I go . . .'

And with that, a final wave and a *'lots of love'*, he's whisked off by his ever-faithful team. Unfortunately my holiday romance with the talented Mr Cowell is over. I wonder if he'll write.

'IF YOU GET A "YES", THEN SHUT UP. THERE ARE TIMES I'VE SAID YES AND THE ARTIST STARTS WITH "I KNEW IT, WE'RE GOING TO DO AMAZING THINGS TOGETHER" AND THE MORE THEY TALK THE MORE I'M THINKING, "I'M REALLY GOING OFF YOU".'

— *Simon Cowell*

SHAMI CHAKRABARTI:
ALL TOGETHER NOW

I AM HAVING COFFEE WITH 'THE most dangerous woman in Britain', according to *The Sun* newspaper. Shami Chakrabarti, former director of Liberty (the human rights lobbying organisation), was given that illustrious title after 9/11 due to her high-profile work in defending civil liberties, or, as *The Sun* saw it, cosying up to terrorists and criminals.

It was a title Shami was happy to accept. *'It was like an honour, better than a CBE from the Queen.'* In a brilliant twist of fate, a few years later Shami found herself helping the journalist who had written the piece. He had been sacked from a radio show for describing a Tory councillor as a 'Nazi' for preventing smokers from being foster parents and his defence was his right to freedom of speech under the Human Rights Act, an act he had so wilfully attacked in the past. But as a protector of everyone's human rights, Shami was there to support him too. It was a situation that illustrated a contradiction that Shami knows only too well. *'We all like having our own human rights, it's just other people's we have a problem with.'*

Unfortunately for Shami, being branded 'dangerous' was the

least she had to deal with in her job: constant racist, misogynistic and personal slurs also came with the territory. But she's not complaining: *'Elsewhere in the world human rights campaigners get physically attacked or worse, so if I have to deal with someone saying nasty things about me in the newspaper or social media then bring it on.'*

The reason why she experienced so much hate was partly the context she was working within. Shami's time at Liberty was shaped by the 9/11 terror attacks and the world's response to them. *'I started at Liberty on the tenth of September. On that first day, I was told to blue-sky think about what our priorities could be. Then the next day happened, so no more blue skies.'* Her role required her to defend very publicly the basic principles of human rights when the world suddenly wanted to ignore them. *'The country did really bad things, not just for human rights, but for our own security: extraordinary renditions, indefinite detention without trial. So I had to say things nobody else wanted to say, and a lot of people didn't want to hear them.'* The scorn of members of the Establishment and the Fourth Estate followed.

She never shirked once, no matter how unpopular her campaigning made her. If anything, she relished the fight, taking on the government over proposed new laws and holding the system to account. I ask her where she gets the resilience to face such strong headwinds and stand up to power. Shami herself attributes it to several things, but none less than her parents. *'I am the daughter of migrants. They'd both been to university in India before moving to England and they raised me to believe I could do anything. I was educated at the local comprehensive and I knew Eton boys were privileged and different, but I never believed they were better than me.'*

She has a personal motto that encapsulates this thinking: *'Anyone's equal, no one's superior.'* It's a principle that guides her approach to life as well as work. *'It's a pretty good way to rub along with other people in the world.'*

The goal of achieving a society where everyone is equal, according to Shami, is still far away. She despairs at how refugees are talked about increasingly with disdain. *'"Refugee" to me is one of the most noble words on the planet. When I grew up in the 1970s we loved refugees because they were Russians who wanted to escape the terrible Soviet bloc for our better way of life. But now we cast refugees as "others", as "less than", as a problem.'* And worse than that, she sees women's place in the world as the biggest inequality going. *'The older I get and the more I see, I think gender injustice is the greatest human rights abuse on the planet. It's literally like an apartheid, except this isn't one country, this is global and millennial and it's insane.'*

She has a one-word answer for tackling such issues of inequality and defending our basic rights, and that is solidarity.

'Powerful elites in the world always succeed by divide and rule, using tools like fear and racism. But solidarity, the basic human connection we can all have with one another, is stronger. It is the magic weapon to achieve change. If we remember that your human rights are the same as my human rights, even if we don't look the same, and if we support one another we all benefit, we all become stronger. Ultimately, we are each other's security.'

THE REAL ARI EMANUEL

I T's Oscar Week and Ari Emanuel, Hollywood super-agent
and inspiration for *Entourage*'s Ari Gold, is a busy man. He's
so busy even his assistant has an assistant, and she's worked
marvels, getting me time with the most powerful man in
Hollywood at Hollywood's busiest time of year. But there isn't a
second to lose.

I'm grabbed from reception and walked quickly, almost at
jogging pace, to his office. A meeting is just ending and this is
our shot. Two people are still being shown out as I am shown in
– we briefly get stuck in the doorway. Inside, Ari is stood at his
chest-high desk, a desk that is placed over a treadmill so he can
work out while he's working. He looks up and over at me, then
to his assistant, and asks, quite reasonably, all things considered, *'So,
who the hell is this guy?'* And so my conversation with Ari begins.

If that makes him sound rude, then it's misleading. Focused, for
sure. Direct, definitely. But not rude. It's just that *'it's a shitty week
for me, what with it being the Oscars, and EVERYONE is in town,
there is a LOT going on'*. He talks in lean, rapid-fire bursts, all protein,
no sugar. A dark-matter magnetism radiates from him; he's unques-
tionably the centre of gravity in the room. He had me at *'So'*.

Ari wants to know why I want him in this book. I explain it's about people at the top of their game, and that he's the most powerful and successful agent in the world. He listens to my answer, reflects for a nanosecond and says, *'That's true. I am.'* And then, a beat later, follows up with, *'Well, it doesn't pay for me to be humble, not in this industry.'*

So what does pay in this industry? What is the secret for getting to the top?

'I've thought about this, and my advice for success comes down to three things: be curious, show up, stay in touch. You have to keep reading, listening, talking, thinking, finding out how people think, what they do. And chase down anything that seems interesting.'

He recounts an article he read ten years ago about a new technology that to him sounded intriguing and to us is now known as virtual reality. So he got on the phone to the person in the piece, invited him for lunch and asked him questions. Ari kept in touch with the guy, sent him the odd email, the occasional article. The same guy called him one Friday night saying that he was off to see some whizz kid he was excited about and asked whether Ari wanted to come along. *'It's 10 p.m. on a Friday night. I'm in bed. It's been a shitty week, pounding away trying to make this place work. But I think, right, fuck it. I get out of bed, put my trousers back on and drive an hour to meet this kid. Best thing I ever did. I loved him, decided to back him, and his company has been a huge success.'*

I say it's easier to be curious, to show up, to stay in touch when you are already successful, when your name opens doors, so I'm keen to understand how he first got going, before his name meant anything. *'Basically I started out by calling the big guys in the agency world back then. I was a nobody, a pimple on their ass, but I just kept calling them and doorstepping them until eventually they gave me an in.'*

I say that it takes a thick skin to keep going in a situation like that. He concedes that's the case and, surprisingly, says that the extreme dyslexia he suffered from as a kid helped him.

'When you're dyslexic you constantly fail, nothing comes easy, so you lose the fear of failing, you get used to being embarrassed. So with cold calling, who gives a shit? They say no, big deal, you just keep calling them till they say yes.'

Furthermore, he says being dyslexic teaches you other things too. It gives you better emotional intelligence: *'You might not be able to read books but you get great at reading people.'* And it teaches you how to put a team together, *'because you can't do everything when you're dyslexic, you need people to help'*. And ironically in an industry typically about 'me', Ari's reputation is for being about the 'we'. The loyalty of his staff seems absolute, as is his to them. As an illustration, one of his colleagues was telling me how, during the terrorist attacks in Paris earlier in the year, as soon as Ari heard the news he got straight on a plane and was there within twenty-four hours, making sure his French team were OK.

Curiosity. Not giving in. Team. All things instrumental to his success.

And it is one of his loyal team members that now gives me the nod. My time is up. As I'm shown out, I take a look back. The last thing I see is Ari going back to his desk, getting back on that treadmill. And thanks to the time he's given me, now busier than ever.

'I'VE THOUGHT ABOUT THIS, AND MY ADVICE FOR SUCCESS COMES DOWN TO THREE THINGS: BE CURIOUS, SHOW UP, STAY IN TOUCH. YOU HAVE TO KEEP READING,

LISTENING, TALKING, THINKING,
FINDING OUT HOW PEOPLE
THINK, WHAT THEY DO.
AND CHASE DOWN ANYTHING
THAT SEEMS INTERESTING.'

– *Ari Emanuel*

MARTHA LANE FOX,
FAIRY GODMOTHER 2.0

I'M IN THE OFFICES OF a hip London digital agency to meet Baroness Martha Lane Fox, the First Lady of the internet. The company is full of people with ironic T-shirts, directional haircuts and piercings that allow you to see through their earlobes. Martha's sitting in the communal coffee bar, looking gloriously countercultural by being dressed in a smart, powder-blue trouser suit. As someone who knows more about digital than all the trendies in London put together, she doesn't need to wear the ripped T-shirt and body piercings to prove it.

As we chat generally, I discover my favourite remarkable fact about Martha. It is not that she was the co-founder of lastminute. com, the dot-com-era-defining start-up that sold for half a unicorn. Nor that she was the youngest female appointee to the House of Lords, impressive though that is. And it is neither the car accident that nearly killed her and resulted in two years confined to a hospital bed as they rebuilt her shattered body, nor that she now runs Doteveryone, her charity focused on making the UK the most digitally advanced nation in the world. Remarkable though these things may be, the nugget that best gives you a sense of the woman is her number of godchildren: she has nineteen. That's two more than Princess Di.

When you meet her, it's not difficult to see why. She is alive with a sense of possibility, potential and optimism. *'I love building things, I love ideas and I love that you can always empower people and improve systems and make things better.'* And her guiding philosophy? *'Without sounding too kooky about it, you feel much better as a person if you default to generosity as opposed to being mean-spirited.'* What lucky godchildren.

Ironically, she herself has not always been on the receiving end of people's better natures. When her friend and co-founder Brent Hoberman floated lastminute.com and the share price crashed, she received more than 2,000 pieces of hate mail, *'including death threats and people calling me every name from B to C'*, as well as business journalists writing in the press that they wished they could shoot her, or that she *'should be put in a burka and told to stay in my box'*. Not much generosity of spirit there. And, tellingly, all that vitriol was focused on her, not her male co-founder.

The lastminute.com story is a time capsule that reflects the internet of the late 1990s. They were ahead of their time, launching in an era before Google even existed. Their original name was LastMinuteNetwork.com but they thought it would be cooler if they dropped that third word. They struggled to raise funds because venture capitalists said people wouldn't buy things over the internet as no one would put their credit card details into a website. It seems laughably naive now, but Martha says it was a different internet back then. *'It was so new and exciting, a real sense the whole world was going to change, we didn't foresee that these huge monopolies like Amazon, Google and Facebook would just go boom and lock down the internet.'*

Her belief in the fundamental power of the internet to help people change things is the driving force behind her organisation Doteveryone, which has the mission to democratise access to and understanding of the internet for, literally, everyone. She is mobilising the government, businesses, schools and communities to ensure everyone has the skills to get online and in a non-curated way: *'No disrespect to Facebook, but the internet is not just Facebook. If you know how to really use the internet, you have access to every opinion, piece of information and tool out there. It can help us all change things.'*

It is this spirit of wanting to improve herself and others, and of seeing the endless possibilities in the world, both online and off, that drives her and it is reflected in the advice she passes on:

'Be bold. If you're bold you might right royally screw up, but you can also achieve much more, so be bold. You've only got your own reputation to lose and that's not important. It's much better to strive for something that seems impossible, that's quite nuts on some level. So be bold, whatever it is. Even if you work on a customer help desk somewhere, ask yourself how can I be bold? Find those small moments of boldness because they are everywhere.'

'BE BOLD. IF YOU'RE BOLD
YOU MIGHT RIGHT ROYALLY
SCREW UP, BUT YOU CAN
ALSO ACHIEVE MUCH MORE, SO
BE BOLD. YOU'VE ONLY GOT
YOUR OWN REPUTATION TO
LOSE AND THAT'S NOT
IMPORTANT. IT'S MUCH BETTER
TO STRIVE FOR SOMETHING
THAT SEEMS IMPOSSIBLE,

THAT'S QUITE NUTS ON SOME
LEVEL. SO BE BOLD, WHATEVER
IT IS. EVEN IF YOU WORK
ON A CUSTOMER HELP DESK
SOMEWHERE, ASK YOURSELF
HOW CAN I BE BOLD? FIND
THOSE SMALL MOMENTS OF
BOLDNESS BECAUSE THEY
ARE EVERYWHERE.'

– *Baroness Martha Lane Fox*

HARRY BELAFONTE,
KINGSMAN

I'M TALKING US POLITICS WITH Harry Belafonte, the eighty-nine-year-old Grammy award-winning singer, titan of the American Civil Rights Movement, and confidant of Martin Luther King. It's a big conversation. He is a man of extraordinary eloquence, intellect and life force, the latter being fuelled by the twin engines of his anger at social injustice and his enduring love of the better side of his country.

We talk about the Republican primaries, which are raging around us while we're in New York. Donald Trump is given short shrift – *'a character clearly smitten with ignorance and arrogance, one doesn't need to linger too long on him'* – but he says what is worth greater consideration is the amount of people responding positively to Trump's messages of hatred, which reveals to Harry the extent to which the American Dream has been corrupted.

Conversely, Harry sees Barack Obama as one of the most intellectually gifted people ever to occupy the office but believes he's endured eight years of the worst animosity of any president in history – a fact that Harry puts down to *'one thing and one thing only. Because he's a man of* colour.'

These two phenomena – Trump's popularity and Obama's received animosity – support his assertion that racism and inequality are alive and rampant in modern-day America and the wider world. And Harry shows no sign of resting while that is still the case. His work extends from fighting AIDS in Africa and serving on the Nuclear Age Peace Foundation to educating American students on the importance of non-violent protest.

Harry Belafonte wasn't born into the worlds of social activism or stardom. Raised in Harlem to working-class parents, his path to a life in the spotlight was precipitated while working as a janitor's assistant in New York. A tenant of his building, short on cash, tipped him with two tickets to the American Negro Theater. Watching the play ignited within Harry a love of the art form and he decided at that moment to become an actor. He signed up for acting lessons and, to pay for them, started singing at night in a New York jazz club. But unexpected success there gave him the opportunity to launch a pop career, popularising Caribbean music through his 'Banana Boat Song (Day-O)', releasing many successful albums of different musical styles and then forging an equally successful film career. All in all, not a bad outcome from a couple of free tickets.

Like many remarkable people he claims his life has been shaped by such moments of happenstance, those chance events none of us have control over. He advises making the most of them. *'The greatest force in my life has been coincidence, and having an openness to receiving whatever the people I met offered and wanted. Due to this my life opened up into a whole set of challenges and joys that I would not have had otherwise.'* He summarises this into one of his main philosophies for living: *'It pays to always answer the knock at the door.'*

With his subsequent fame came considerably more of those knocks, including one that turned out to be the most significant of all. From a young pastor by the name of Martin Luther King, asking for Harry's help at one of his events. And at that first meeting *'Dr King called me to help him with his mission, and there I was caught up in a social movement that changed the American political landscape and the global family.'* He became Dr King's mentor and provider, supporting Dr King's family, bailing him out when he got arrested, financing the Freedom Rides, and organising the March on Washington, and he has been carrying the torch for the Civil Rights Movement and other social injustices ever since. *'Those guys left me with my hands full.'*

So, given all that he has stood for, fought for, and seen his friends die for, it makes sense that his greatest piece of advice is this:

> *'Discover the joy of embracing diversity. When people become more open to the strange, to the unusual, to the radical, to the "other", we become more nourished as a species. Currently our ability to do that is being manipulated, diversity is being looked upon as a source of evil rather than as a source of joy and development. We must recapture the profound benefits of seeing the joy in our collective diversity, not the fear.'*

The most important advice I ever heard.

'DISCOVER THE JOY OF EMBRACING DIVERSITY. WHEN PEOPLE BECOME MORE OPEN TO THE STRANGE, TO THE UNUSUAL, TO THE RADICAL, TO THE "OTHER", WE BECOME MORE NOURISHED AS A SPECIES. CURRENTLY OUR ABILITY TO DO THAT IS BEING MANIPULATED,

DIVERSITY IS BEING LOOKED
UPON AS A SOURCE OF EVIL
RATHER THAN AS A SOURCE OF
JOY AND DEVELOPMENT.
WE MUST RECAPTURE THE
PROFOUND BENEFITS OF
SEEING THE JOY IN OUR
COLLECTIVE DIVERSITY,
NOT THE FEAR.'

– Harry Belafonte

SANDI TOKSVIG,
SERIOUSLY FUNNY

THERE'S A RAINBOW FLAG KNOTTED around the large brass door handle of the Soho-based club I'm about to enter – a show of solidarity for the victims of the Orlando massacre at a gay nightclub just twelve hours before. It's a terrible event that has horrified everyone and has a deep, personal relevance to Sandi Toksvig, the much-loved writer, actress, producer and comedian. She came out as the first openly gay woman in UK public life in the 1990s and was subject to extreme homophobia. *'I had death threats and stalkers and people sectioned. But you don't have to be in the public eye to be afraid. Blind hatred is scary for anybody.'*

In her case, the biggest outpouring of vitriol was reserved for the fact that (thanks to a sperm-donating friend) Sandi and her partner were mothers to three children. The *Daily Mail* ran the headline 'If God Meant Lesbians to Have Children He Would Have Made It Possible'. Members of the religious right wrote and said they were going to kill her on God's behalf. *'Because apparently God was busy and needed them to help pick up the slack.'* Fortunately, she says, things are much better these days: *'People are very nice to me, I get hugged in the street a lot. I don't know why. I think it's because I'm small.'*

.This is part of what makes Sandi unique: she can be simultaneously funny and extremely serious. She loves comedy – *'it's a nice thing, people can forget about their mortgage and marital troubles and come and laugh'* – but she is driven by a more serious motivation than just providing entertainment: *'I have no drive for fame, no drive for money, I couldn't give a damn about either of those things, I'm not in the least bit religious, but I do have a drive to make a difference. I'm only here this one time and I intend to make it count.'*

Her most recent manifestation of this credo was co-founding the newest political party in the UK, the Women's Equality Party, an organisation with the specific aim of bringing gender equality to education, employment, social welfare, culture and every other aspect of society. Sandi says it started as an idea on stage at a women's rights festival, but once they'd thought up the concept she couldn't leave it alone. *'You have to get off your arse and do something, don't you? I will not go to my grave thinking I didn't try.'*

There's no fear of that. The party already has more than 20,000 members, has fielded two candidates in the recent London mayor campaign and will be putting forward representatives at the next general election.

It leads me to a more pragmatic question: given all the presenting, writing and acting jobs she already has, how does she balance it all? Her answer is equally pragmatic: *'I work very hard and I get up very early. People say how do you get everything done? The answer is you just have to spend lots of hours.'*

And this appetite for work relates to her most valuable piece of advice:

> *'Just work hard and be passionate. If I've taught my kids one thing, it's to be passionate. I'm passionate about food, my friends, my wife, passionate about our house, our dog. I'm passionate. I get up and I'm passionate – my father believed in it and that's the one thing he taught me, that life is amazing and it's full of people you haven't met yet, music you haven't heard, books you haven't read. And if you start each day looking for something to be passionate about, mostly you won't be disappointed because every day you'll find something that'll make you say, look at that, that's so cool.'*

On that manifesto for life, we want Sandi Toksvig for prime minister.

'Get off your arse

and do something.'

– Sandi Toksvig

THE LESSER SPOTTED
SIR DAVID ATTENBOROUGH

ALL I CAN HEAR ARE the sounds of nature. The air is filled with mysterious chirpings and squawks, exotic whistles, tocks and clicks. In quick succession, a Ghanaian Giant Squeaker Frog, a Madagascan Side-Necked Turtle and a Pakistani Snow Leopard dart past in front of me. Then a Papua New Guinea warrior in tribal headdress appears. Our eyes meet. He gives me a friendly smile and comes towards me, extending his hand in a traditional greeting. And I think, not bad for a Tuesday evening in West London.

Admittedly the sounds are recorded and the animals are on film, but the warrior is very much real and enjoying both his first trip to London and his first-ever gin and tonic. We're at the Whitley Awards for Nature, an Oscar-lite awards ceremony for rising stars in the world of conservation. The venue is the Royal Geographical Society, an appropriate choice given the far-flung origins of tonight's nominees, each of which has dedicated their life to defending their threatened native species. The Ghanaian chap protecting the Giant Squeaker Frogs has even learnt to mimic their mating call and does so loudly when collecting his prize. It makes for a memorable acceptance speech.

While the evening is shaped around celebrating these conservationists and their projects, the biggest draw of the night is guest of honour and the world's most revered naturalist Sir David Attenborough. He's dressed on-brand in a crumpled cream linen suit, looking for all the world like someone who has just come back from exotic travels, which of course he has. He's at the event to support the conservationists and wants no limelight for himself. Like his documentary subjects, he seems more comfortable hiding in the long grass and remains in the audience, avoiding the stage.

To talk to him one-on-one, he is the charismatic yet humble man you would imagine him to be. He says he gives time to these awards every year, including narrating each of the conservation project's films, because *'local people with local knowledge and a vested interest'* do the best conservation work and *'it's more important than ever to support those who protect the planet'*. It's lost on no one that the room is full of people inspired to do just that because of the films Sir David has made. The effect is global: President Obama credits Sir David with awakening his fascination in the natural world as a boy and asked Sir David to the White House to pick his brains on conservation and fulfil a childhood ambition of getting to hang out with Nature's commander-in-chief.

According to Sir David, the growing encroachment by man on our natural habitat and the ever-increasing demands we place on the environment has got progressively worse over his sixty years of film-making. And he's clear-sighted about the fundamental driver of the issue: *'there's no major problem facing our planet that would not be easier to solve with fewer people'*.

He also underlines the importance of appreciating what is around us: not just our natural history, although that is of course of fundamental importance, but also our art, other people too. He recommends what he calls an *'explorer's mentality'*, delighting in and savouring all the riches of life as we journey through it. And while doing so heeds *'it's a good idea to create more than you consume'*.

There's also a boyish mischievousness about him. When I ask for his best piece of advice, he feigns ignorance and says he's never been able to think of anything clever to say his whole life, and then winks. When I push a second time for his most valuable advice, he continues in the vein of what he has been saying about appreciating the miracle of what life on earth has to offer, and it fits exactly with the endless fascination he exhibits in every second of his films:

> *'I have never met a child that is not fascinated by our natural world, the animal kingdom and the wonders within it. It is only as we get older that we sometimes lose that sense of wonderment. But I think we would all be better off if we kept it. So my advice is to never lose that, do what you can to always keep that sense of magic with our natural world alive.'*

And no one does that better than Sir David.

❖

'I HAVE NEVER MET A CHILD
THAT IS NOT FASCINATED
BY OUR NATURAL WORLD,
THE ANIMAL KINGDOM AND
THE WONDERS WITHIN IT.
IT IS ONLY AS WE GET
OLDER THAT WE SOMETIMES
LOSE THAT SENSE OF

WONDERMENT. BUT I THINK
WE WOULD ALL BE BETTER
OFF IF WE KEPT IT. SO MY
ADVICE IS TO NEVER LOSE
THAT, DO WHAT YOU CAN TO
ALWAYS KEEP THAT SENSE OF
MAGIC WITH OUR NATURAL
WORLD ALIVE.'

– *Sir David Attenborough*

GETTING STOCIOUS
WITH DAME JUDI DENCH

I'VE NEVER FELT WORSE ON a beautiful summer's morning. It's Friday, 24 June 2016, and the UK has just voted to come out of the EU. I stayed up all night watching the results with the campaign team I've been part of for the last six months, realising with a deepening sense of unease that the country has chosen to burn bridges and build walls instead.

Such thoughts are my mental backdrop as I drive to visit Dame Judi Dench at her home in deepest, greenest Surrey. On the way, I pass a multitude of red 'Vote Leave' posters, reminding me that at least half the people in the country will be waking up happy this morning. Dame Judi Dench is not one of them.

I find her in her garden. She's dressed in white clothes and sunlight, sat by an old friend of a table in the middle of her lawn, safeguarded by reassuringly seasoned trees and the crumbly walls of her gorgeous house. She asks how I am. I bypass forty-three years of ingrained Britishness and reply honestly, explain-ing that I'm unbelievably depressed by what's happened. *'Me too,'* she replies. *'There's nothing else for it, I'm going to get stocious.'*

'Stocious?' I ask, confused by the unfamiliar but respectable-sounding term. 'Yes, stocious. It's an old Irish word. My mother was from Dublin. It means being drunk, but even more so.' I guess I was wrong about the respectable part.

We've not met before this encounter, but a shared sense of grief bonds us. We huddle together at the table, taking it in turns to bemoan the loss of identity and tolerance we feel the outcome represents. We're as bad as each other, and wallow communally for a while before pulling ourselves back up into the light.

I end up spending three hours with Dame Judi. She is everything you would imagine her to be: thoughtful, candid, warm, funny, kind, the spirit of solace manifested as a person. Over the course of our conversation we graduate from sipping iced coffee to drinking champagne, but I leave neither stocious nor, thanks to Dame Judi, feeling the need any more to be so.

I do, however, leave intoxicated from the delicious cocktail of advice, anecdotes and affirmation she serves up. My favourite story is of the time eight years ago when she received a bad review from the theatre critic Charles Spencer. 'He didn't just criticise my performance, he also listed other things he thought I'd not done well. And that irritated me. So one night I woke up and thought, I'm going to write to him and get it off my chest. So I did. I wrote, "Dear Charles Spencer, I used to quite admire you, I now think you are a total shit," and sent it off.'

Like all good stories, there's a second half. Earlier this year, Dame Judi was at the Critics' Circle Awards. 'I felt a tap on my shoulder and a man said, "My name is Charles Spencer, I crave your forgiveness," and I said, "Then you may kiss my boot." And he did, he *got down on the floor and kissed my boot. He then got up and exclaimed, "I'm so relieved." But I said, "I haven't said I forgive you," and I walked away.'* Pause for dramatic effect. *'I wrote to him the next day and said, of course, "I forgive you." But it was very rectifying.'*

Funnily enough, she never intended to be the subject of acting reviews. Her plan was to be a theatre designer and that's what she studied, *'but my older brother always wanted to be an actor and I caught it off him like measles'*. And it was her other brother who introduced her to Shakespeare. *'I was six years old and went to see him play Duncan in* Macbeth, *and he came on and said, "What bloody man is that?" And I thought this is it, he's sworn and he's allowed to stand up there and say it, so after that I used to say "What bloody man is that?" all the time, knowing I could get away with it.'*

Her talk of Shakespeare leads to something remarkable happening, for me at least. Dame Judi puts her head back and launches into a heart-stopping recital of the Bard: 'For once upon a raw and gusty day, the troubled Tiber chafing with her shores, Caesar said to me, "Darest thou, Cassius, now, leap with me into this . . ."' She is momentarily transported to the shores of the Tiber, and she's taken me with her. It occurs to me, I'm getting a private one-on-one performance of Shakespeare by Judi Dench while drinking her champagne. In your dreams, Charles Spencer.

She advises me on the importance of having passions. Hers is most definitely Shakespeare. And with the way she delivers it, virtually breathes it, if he were alive the feeling would be mutual. When she became an actor, Shakespeare was all she wanted to do. Her very first role was playing Ophelia at the Old Vic, which caused controversy, as it was unheard of for an unknown to bag a lead part on their first try. But she, of course, delivered and hasn't stopped doing so since.

She surprises me, though, by saying that the nerves are greater now than back then. *'The more you know, the more unsure you get. At first you don't know the pitfalls. But if I didn't have nerves I'd be worried, as they engender energy, they're petrol.'*

She says a theatre performance still leaves her feeling raw and exposed. *'I am like that frog you'd see in biology class at school, split down the middle and pinned out, ready to be dissected. I just want someone to come in and give me a hug and be positive, but people knock on the door and come in and say things like, "We had the most terrible journey down from Gloucester."'*

It is a small example of her bigger point, that life is better if you stay positive.

> **'If I was passing on anything, I would say, for goodness sake, look for the pluses in life. Being negative completely erodes everything. If something bad happens, I always say cancel and continue and get back on track. There's no good being negative, I don't believe in negativity.'**

Then one beat later.

> **'Except in regard to the referendum.'**

I'll drink to that.

'LOOK FOR THE PLUSES
IN LIFE. BEING NEGATIVE
COMPLETELY ERODES
EVERYTHING. IF SOMETHING
BAD HAPPENS, I ALWAYS SAY
CANCEL AND CONTINUE AND
GET BACK ON TRACK.'

– Dame Judi Dench

SQUADDIE BANTER WITH
CORPORAL ANDY REID

'*A*re *me family jewels still intact?*' That was Corporal
Andy Reid's first question when he regained consciousness after standing on a Taliban IED, which blew off
both his legs and one arm, ten days before the end of his tour
in Afghanistan as a British Army infantryman. Fortunately for
Andy, his future wife Claire and now their son William, the answer
was a resounding yes.

He tells me this when I meet him in his hometown. He has
kindly collected me from the station, rolling by in his pimped-up
4x4 Jeep, with tinted windows, spoilers, the works. This is no
typical disability vehicle, and Andy's is no typical story.

Back in his kitchen, while he deftly one-handedly makes tea
for us both, Andy recounts the time his parents first came to see
him in hospital after he was evacuated from Afghanistan. Finding
their son in bed, missing both legs and an arm, and with the
remaining one in plaster, his dad, not knowing what else to do,
patted Andy on the head. *'I said, "I'm not a fucking dog, Dad," and
as soon as I said that we all started laughing and we knew then, it is
going to be OK.'*

To Andy, the jokes are 'squaddie banter', the humour that soldiers use to lighten the mood and bring a bit of normality to situations that are often anything but. *'Four weeks after the accident, I went on a Remembrance Parade, and it was really cold, so I said to the boys, "It's bloody freezing, I can hardly feel my toes." It made everyone crack up and removed any awkwardness.'*

The last thing Andy wants is people stepping on eggshells around him or feeling sorry for him. *'I joined up and I accept responsibility for what's happened to me, I knew the risks. That's helped me move on a lot easier. You don't move on very far by blaming someone else every time, it's just going to make you depressed and angry and bitter.'* It's a way of thinking that shows the resilience and determination that makes Andy such a role-model soldier.

Instead of being bitter, each year Andy celebrates the day of the explosion. He calls it Happy Being Alive Day. *'When I woke up in hospital I realised I wasn't a victim, I was a survivor. Six of the guys from my company all died from one IED. I got to leave hospital after two weeks and go home, they didn't.'* He says he needs to honour those fellow soldiers who weren't lucky enough to come back by living his life to the fullest rather than sitting around feeling sorry for himself.

One piece of advice he passes on to other people dealing with such a life-changing challenge is to remember that *'the body will achieve what the mind believes'*. On each Happy Being Alive Day he sets himself a goal to do something physically challenging to prove he can do it. With this attitude he has so far climbed Snowdon, run a 10k race, cycled most of Britain and skydived twice, all things people would assume were out of the picture but which Andy willed into reality.

This spirit of keeping going is evident in the giant poster he has displayed high up on his kitchen wall. It features a photo of Winston Churchill and one of his famous quotes in large type: 'If you're going through hell, then keep going.' The poster also makes it clear that Andy's journey has been extremely tough. He says not being able to run around with his little boy can really get to him and the pain can be gruesome on occasion, but he is resolute in his attitude of just keeping going. *'My little boy isn't going to benefit from having some dad mope about the house, is he?'*

He talks about his new life after the army. He is a man with a lot going on. He's a successful writer, with one book telling his story already out and another on the way. He's opened a café and bar in his local town, he got married, he's in-demand as a public speaker on coping with adversity, and, most importantly to Andy, he can be around more for his young son, something that being in the army would not have allowed.

It's this new life and these achievements that give the context to his most important piece of advice:

> *'At the end of the day I think the most important thing is don't look back on what has happened. Instead look forward to what you can do. Just crack on.'*

He is a living, breathing, walking five-star example of that philosophy.

And his final comment underlines the benefit of his approach in the most indelible way. *'You know, if somebody said to me tomorrow, "Andy, do you want your legs back and the life you were living before?" I'd say, "No, thanks. I'm happier as I am now."'*

'THE MOST IMPORTANT THING
IS DON'T LOOK BACK ON WHAT
HAS HAPPENED. INSTEAD LOOK
FORWARD TO WHAT YOU CAN
DO. JUST CRACK ON.'

— *Corporal Andy Reid*

SIR RICHARD BRANSON,
ISLAND MAN

I FIRST MET SIR RICHARD BRANSON at his old house in Oxfordshire, where he was hosting a festival-sized party in the adjoining fields for his Virgin Atlantic staff. He was the inverse of the Great Gatsby, stood at the gate, greeting every person that came in, all 15,000 of them. For over four hours he shook hands, kissed cheeks, welcoming all – the embodiment of one of his management principles: *if you look after your people, they will look after you.*

These days, the place where Virgin staff dream of meeting the boss is at his official home on Necker, his family's private island, which nestles among the baby-blue waters of the Caribbean Sea. Every year, a few lucky Virgin employees get invited. As perks go, it beats free tea and coffee.

I'm on the island for a week, not as staff but as a (very grateful) friend of the family. I can attest that whoever coined the phrase 'it's better to travel than to arrive' hadn't been to Necker. Even the journey here is epic. You fly by propeller plane to a nearby landing strip and board one of several speedboats, full of friendly crew, loud sounds and chilled drinks, skimming over azure seas and nipping between islands until you get to the very last one in the archipelago, Necker.

When you see it, you can see why God kept Necker till last: two perfect crescents of virgin white, palm-fringed beach, trailing off either side of a verdant headland, upon which the proud main house inevitably sits. And while photos online might prepare you for the beachside jacuzzis hued from natural rock and calming infinity pools staring out at untroubled seas, what you don't expect is the overwhelming beauty of the wildlife: skies chaotic with bright birds of paradise, lemurs' screeching calls for a suitable mate, an inland lagoon 300 pink flamingoes deep. I say this as a fussy, hard-to-please person – the place is literally perfect. It is where God would take his holidays.

It also affords an opportunity to observe one of the world's most revered entrepreneurs up close in his natural habitat. And if there is one behaviour, beyond the generosity and affability of this rare breed of business titan that stands out, it is the sheer dedication of the man to get the most from life, treating every hour as precious, a one-off gift to savour.

And if you don't believe me, this is his typical day on Necker:

6 a.m. Tennis with hot female tennis coach from Miami
8 a.m. Yoga on the terrace with resident teacher
8.30 a.m. Breakfast with wife, children, grandchildren and friends
9 a.m. Kitesurf round the other island he owns (he's now bought the one opposite Necker too because one island is never enough) with son and son-in-law
10 a.m. Head to private office with resident personal assistant

and broadcast quality media studio to support the countless Virgin business and charitable initiatives across the world

1 p.m. Zipwire down from main house to beach BBQ with family and friends

2 p.m. Poolside chess with whoever is feeling brave enough (winner: Branson, R.)

3 p.m. Golf buggy back to main house to work

4 p.m. Second tennis session with hot coach

5.30 p.m. Feed lemurs

6 p.m. Necker tennis tournament with other guests (winner: Branson, R.)

8 p.m. Dinner by the pool

9 p.m. Party in the main house

All this is done with a flip-flop-wearing infectious enthusiasm. It's like he's woken up that morning and to his great surprise and delight found himself in this amazing paradise, forgetting the fact that he's the one who spent thirty years creating it.

Over those same thirty years, he's also redefined the nature of business. Before Branson came along, the stereotype of an entrepreneur in the UK was a wheeling-dealing Del Boy type. Branson changed that. He made setting up a business seem sexy, cool, fun. And, most importantly of all, possible. His success, life and approach to business underwrites the ambitions of other entrepreneurs, providing a licence to dream, to think 'what if'.

I catch him at one of the beach bars, at his feet the kitesurfing board he used to get there. He's talking with the bar girl making the drinks. He finds out she's going back to the UK but is worried about her lack of work. So he starts making calls, offering to help get her a job. It reminds me of a time when I was one of the judges alongside him on a young entrepreneurs competition. As we debated who should win, he made sure extra money was found so everyone would get something. The man is relentlessly helpful. The answer is always positive. His informal title in his own organisation is Head of Yes; his most famous words, *'Screw it, let's do it.'*

But when I ask for his most valuable piece of advice, it is not specifically about work and business, but about life and how to live it. Maybe it is the Eden-like setting we're in, or more likely it's because he follows his own advice that we're in this island of earthly delights:

> *'People talk about work and play as if they are separate things, with one being there to compensate for the other, but all of it is life, all of it is precious. Don't waste any of it doing something you don't want to do. And do all of it with the people you love.'*

As he says this, I can see in the distance, one by one, his family, friends and PA zipwiring down from the headland to join him on his private beach for another lunch in the sun. And I think to myself for the hundredth time, this man knows how to live.

'ALL OF IT IS LIFE, ALL OF IT IS PRECIOUS. DON'T WASTE ANY OF IT DOING SOMETHING YOU DON'T WANT TO DO. AND DO ALL OF IT WITH THE PEOPLE YOU LOVE.'

– Sir Richard Branson

KATIE PIPER,
SUPER ROLE MODEL

I T's A SUNNY AFTERNOON IN London and I'm in a posh
bar drinking G&Ts with the gorgeous model, TV presenter,
philanthropist and best-selling author Katie Piper. It's a tough
life.

Over the drinks, I learn many remarkable things about my
cocktail buddy: the thousands of people she has helped with her
charity; her prolific output as a writer, publishing five books in
just eight years; her ability to juggle her many work commitments
with the demands of being a parent. And the most remarkable
thing of all, her approach to life since the day, eight years ago,
when she was raped by her ex-boyfriend and had sulphuric acid
thrown in her face.

It was an attack designed to do as much physical harm as
possible and in that regard it was horribly successful. After waking
from an induced twelve-day coma her doctor explained the
situation, which in summary was: you're blind in both eyes, you
have no face left, you're struggling to breathe because you've
swallowed your oesophagus and the police are here to video you
in case you don't survive until the trial.

Her immediate response was simple and understandable: *'I just thought to myself, "I'll do whatever I need to do to get discharged and then quietly go home, take an overdose and kill myself."'* The following weeks passed slowly: bedridden, in pain, unable to move, with a nurse present twenty-four hours a day, Katie would silently plan her suicide. But one night when thinking about how to do it, *'something, somewhere said to me: "Don't kill yourself. I can't tell you why, but there's a bigger reason. You have to stay alive."'* In that moment, she says, she made what became the most important decision of her life: she chose to be a survivor, not a victim.

That resolve hardened when the time came to be discharged from hospital. She praises the brilliant care she received from the nurses and doctors looking after her, but when people started talking about disability benefits and council flats, she realised just how low expectations were of what her life would become. *'No one said a disfigured woman can still get married, have babies, be sexy, be a CEO, be a trailblazer, be a leader in fashion. So I decided to go out there and reach for everything I wanted. As far as everyone else was concerned I had nothing to lose anyway.'*

Part of the recipe of building her new life was acceptance of what had happened. *'I said to myself, I'm never going to look like the old me or Cindy Crawford, but maybe I could be my own kind of beautiful.'* Another part was sheer resilience. *'If you look around at all the things that have been achieved, they were usually done by people told there was no hope at all, but they carried on plugging away regardless. I took inspiration from that.'* And of course there was a huge degree of bravery, of enduring more than forty operations and skin grafts, of withstanding wearing a mask twenty-three hours a day, of facing the outside world again for the first time. *'In the early days I didn't want to leave the house, I was really agoraphobic, they were dark times. But there came a point where I'd been watching* Loose Women *for a year, wearing pyjamas, and I needed to get out.'*

As a single woman who aspired to get married and start a family there was also the world of dating to tackle. *'I was living in a one-bed flat in Chiswick in a plastic face mask just trying to get someone to text back, and I thought OK, for all my positivity, this is quite difficult, no one is going to fancy me.'* But she wasn't going to let her disability get in the way of what she wanted – to be a mother. *'I started putting money aside to freeze my eggs and started researching how to adopt a child because as far as I was concerned nothing was going to stop me becoming a mum.'* In the end she kept going with the dating and did meet a guy, fall in love, get married and have a child. And there are the glamorous *Hello!* features to prove it.

Katie Piper says people typically just assume disabilities put you at a disadvantage, but she wasn't prepared to accept that. *'People assumed my life was over. I didn't. On paper I should have less opportunities and be unhappy. I should be clinically depressed and dependent on alcohol. But I've never been more positive, and I've never attracted so many positive, successful people into my life.'*

Those things people automatically thought would no longer apply to her – getting married, becoming a mum, returning to modelling, running a charity, helping thousands of other burn sufferers – she's done all of them and more. The insight she's got from these achievements and her experience over the last eight years inform her best piece of advice:

'The whole thing has taught me that the barriers we put before ourselves don't really exist. The only way barriers exist is in our heads. We create them, we feed them, and we choose to keep them alive. So we can also choose to break them down. Confidence and happiness are not luck or something only other people can have, they are decisions you make that involve hard work, commitment and believing that you actually deserve it. There are no barriers to stop you getting them. And if for whatever reason you ever feel in despair, it is worth remembering God gives his toughest journeys to his strongest soldiers.'

'THE ONLY WAY BARRIERS
EXIST IS IN OUR HEADS. WE
CREATE THEM, WE FEED THEM,
AND WE CHOOSE
TO KEEP THEM ALIVE.'

– *Katie Piper*

MIKE BLOOMBERG,
NEW YORK'S FINEST

O NE OF THE MOST REMARKABLE things about remarkable people is that once they defy the odds by
becoming successful in one area, they often go and
do the same in an entirely different one.

Mike Bloomberg is the quintessential example.

In his thirties he starts Bloomberg from scratch and grows it
into a global media company, becoming in the process the four-
teenth richest person in the world. That is pretty good going.
Then he sidesteps into politics and becomes the most successful
mayor of all time, presiding over the capital city of the world,
New York City, for an unmatched three terms.

When you meet him in person, it quickly becomes evident
that he is the human manifestation of the city he led. Brusque,
busy, not big on sleep.

He has a reputation for talking fast. And he does. But he is
a man who likes to get things done and get them done early.
As mayor he committed the city to reducing its greenhouse
gas emissions by 30 per cent by 2030, then delivered 19 per
cent in just six years. He launched a project to plant a million

new trees in New York by 2017: it was completed two years early.

And, like the city, he constantly reinvents himself. He was originally a registered Democrat, but then stood for mayor as a Republican, using his own money to fund his campaign so he was beholden to no one. As a Republican, he was pro-choice, pro-gun laws and pro-immigration reform. All the things, as a Republican, you're not supposed to be. And then when he stood for his third term as New York mayor, which technically you couldn't even do (but the city council voted to change the rules to allow him to do so), he stood as an Independent, and won.

Then, after this political career, he next gets busy with philanthropy, giving over $1.8 billion to more than 850 charities. A self-made man with a deep-seated belief in the importance of helping others, funding everything from building new hospitals and tackling climate change to further education.

In short, the man does not stop.

What's his best advice on how to lead such a full, successful, busy life?

'Well, to get anywhere, you've got to work hard, so that means you've got to do something that you love. Who wants a life where you turn up each day to do something you don't like? But most importantly, make sure you actually then get up and do it. There is always someone else who can do what you can do, so you've got to make sure you do it first, before the other guy does. You have to get up early every morning and get to it.'

In other words, the mayor of the city that never sleeps says, 'Wake up!'

'THERE IS ALWAYS SOMEONE ELSE WHO CAN DO WHAT YOU CAN DO, SO YOU'VE GOT TO MAKE SURE YOU DO IT FIRST.'

– *Mike Bloomberg*

THE UNCONVENTIONAL
DIANA ATHILL

I'M IN A NORTH LONDON home for retired ladies, an old crumble-bricked mansion house in the backstreets of Highgate. There's a warmth and cosiness to the quietness of the corridors I am tentatively wandering along, as I wonder which door the lady I am here to visit resides behind. I have an appointment with ninety-seven-year-old Diana Athill, someone regarded as London's finest editor during her fifty-year publishing career, when she edited everyone from Jack Kerouac to Philip Roth, and who, now in her nineties, has become a prize-winning writer herself. And, for today at least, an imparter of remarkable relationship advice.

I manage to avoid the scandal of walking unannounced into some retired lady's bedroom and find a member of staff who takes me to Diana's modest living quarters. From her first words, it is clear that I am with someone who has led no ordinary life – and who has no ordinary things to say. The first topic is sex and infidelity, not what one expects when visiting genteel ladies in their retirement homes. I settle back in my chair. This is going to be a big conversation. *'If you are married, you cannot expect a lifetime of anyone being totally faithful. Or if you do, you are mad. I*

–

wouldn't want someone who fucked everything he saw, but infidelity happens and it's daft to collapse a marriage over it.'

While not everyone would agree with such a strong view, it is inarguable that Diana practises what she preaches. Her longest relationship was with the Jamaican playwright Barry Reckord. They met in their forties but after eight years with Diana he began to have an affair with a woman from his theatre. When Diana realised it was serious, she suggested that the mistress move in. The three lived together amicably for many years. It is not most people's idea of romance, but it is a story with a happy, albeit unconventional, ending: the woman in question remains Diana's best friend to this day.

It is actually romance that Diana advises people to be wary of when starting a relationship. She says people get a kick out of being romantic, of being passionately in love at the beginning of an affair, and that's how they choose their partners, but the feeling never endures. And you then risk ending up with *'one of those ghastly marriages you see; chaps sitting in restaurants with their wives, neither of them exchanging a single word'*. For a woman of letters, not having anything to say to your partner is the worst fate imaginable. Instead, you should look for a partner with whom you can say anything to each other, who you have a lot in common with, who you are interested in, where you both hold the same things dear. *'When you find that, it is not a particularly romantic feeling but it is a very, very comfortable feeling, it makes for a better long-term relationship.'*

The longer I listen, the more I begin to understand her point. Typically, people think that one person should be able to satisfy all our needs – friendship, intimacy, passion. But the person that proves to be the best companion may not be the best lover. If so, according to Diana, there is nothing wrong with having sex with someone else if you need a bit of extra excitement. *'When I was getting on, I needed the thrill of a new person. It was a nice, once-a-week meeting to get me going. But that was not at all a romantic affair and I wouldn't have wanted to be married to him. I was fond of him, he was a lovely old boy, but it was just sex.'*

These are very modern views. The fact that they are being advocated by a lady in her late nineties who grew up in a more rigid era makes them all the more remarkable and shows how unconventional Diana truly is. Her best piece of advice remains absolutely on message.

> **'Do not be possessive. It is one of the most dangerous things, especially in relation to sex. There are a lot of people who think it's indecent to not be possessive when you are married. I think it's fatal. Don't let your passion trap you into trying to own the person. The trick is to love them, not to possess them.'**

And her lifetime of knowledge and experience makes her feel compelled to add: *'And if they are unfaithful, forgiving them normally turns out to be what works.'*

'Do not be possessive. It is
one of the most dangerous
things, especially in
relation to sex. There are
a lot of people who think
it's indecent to not be
possessive when you

ARE MARRIED. I THINK IT'S
FATAL. DON'T LET YOUR
PASSION TRAP YOU INTO
TRYING TO OWN THE PERSON.
THE TRICK IS TO LOVE THEM,
NOT TO POSSESS THEM.'

— *Diana Athill*

ANDY MURRAY,
DROUGHT BREAKER

I S THERE A SPORT TOUGHER to master professionally than tennis? The brutal training schedules that start in childhood and don't stop till you retire; your life constantly on the road, away from family and friends; the very nature of the game itself: a modern-day duel, one person pitted against another, no teammates to share the load; hours of battling, day after day under intense scrutiny; and the mathematically illogical, maddening truth that even though a match can involve over 250 points, each point can prove disproportionately significant. Tennis is arguably the purest, hardest, most unforgiving of all the sports.

Then imagine if you have decided to take all that on, decided to shape your life around the sheer unlikeliness of making it as a pro, turned down the tempting football training contract you're offered at an early age and foregone all other paths through life. Just as your hard work and sacrifices start to pay off and you rise up through the ranks, thanks to a quirk of fate it turns out that your time coincides with not one but three kings dominating at the highest level, a cartel of tennis Dons each showing unprecedented levels of success, skills and consistency. Knowing that in any other period of time your own talents and mastery would make you champion many times over, but the universe has served you a dodgy line-call just when it counts, what do you do?

If you're Andy Murray, you take it on the chin and do what you have always done: get back to work and keep practising, keep improving. You get forensic with your technique. Break everything down to the smallest detail, work out how you can get the most from each muscle, each meal, each mind technique. Somehow you absorb and redirect the extraordinary pressure of expectation, channelling that energy instead into chasing every ball.

And the result? You become that fourth king – starting with Olympic Gold, then that first Grand Slam victory at the US Open, then, on the fifth championship point, the most coveted title in tennis, if not sport: Wimbledon. The Holy Grail. You become the nation's rain-maker, ending a seventy-seven-year drought for the country. Then three years later, with the British public fragile and fractious from months of bad news, a second Wimbledon victory, playing better than ever before, and the world begins to think, maybe you're just getting started.

So there is probably no one alive who means and fundamentally inhabits his own words of advice more than Andy Murray:

'Always believe that when you apply yourself, you can achieve anything. Make sure you give 100 per cent and work as hard as you can in everything you do, not just in what you

enjoy but also in life. And don't forget, natural ability will only get you so far, there is no substitute for practice.'

From the guy who turned practice into perfect.

'ALWAYS BELIEVE THAT WHEN YOU APPLY YOURSELF, YOU CAN ACHIEVE ANYTHING . . . DON'T FORGET, NATURAL ABILITY WILL ONLY GET YOU SO FAR, THERE IS NO SUBSTITUTE FOR PRACTICE.'

– Andy Murray

❖

DR MAKI MANDELA'S SHOES

The first time I meet Dr Maki Mandela, eldest surviving child of Nelson Mandela and his wife Evelyn Mase, is at a charity dinner held in honour of the men imprisoned alongside her father. It is an emotional event. The night is to celebrate her father's and his comrades' success in winning freedom for South Africa, but it is tinged with sadness for the price they, their families and countless others paid for it. On stage Dr Mandela, resplendently dressed in South African national dress, talks candidly and beautifully about her father, throughout it all remaining strong and serene, a daughter any father would be proud of.

When I meet her later, one-on-one, it becomes clear this inner strength and calm extends to not suffering fools gladly. I can tell because I am the fool: I'm a little nervous and my unclear, rushed introduction is given short shrift. *'So what is it you want to hear from me?'* is her curt response.

I explain I'm interested in her philosophy on life. Fortunately, it is a question that chimes with her.

'With hindsight I've learnt that all strength and power comes from within. Over the years I've dealt with my inner demons, my bitterness,

my anger, to look at myself, to take a step to be a better Maki, to live authentically.'

The anger she refers to was largely in response to the absence of her father from an early age. 'We had a love–hate relationship. At times I resented the fact that I had lost him to prison.' She talks openly about the reality of her father, the man. 'I know my dad as my dad. I know him with feet of clay. I've seen him in his glory, where he would walk tall, when he would bow to no man, and I've seen him in the last years of his life when he was sickly and bedridden, and he was dignified until the end. But I know he is flesh and blood, he was like you and me.'

She, of course, still respected him. 'He was very focused. If he said he was going somewhere – it didn't matter what was on that road – he went there. He lived authentically, and true to himself – that's what I admire about my dad.'

Obviously, living in the shadow of a man revered by the world was not easy, something that even Mandela himself acknowledged. 'He always advocated me finding my own path in life. He knew I could not fit in his shoes. He said if your mission is to be the same as your parents, then you have no ambition.'

Her own path was to become a social worker, PhD anthropologist, businesswoman and vineyard-owning entrepreneur – finding her own way through life, independent of her father's shadow while loving him for who he was.

It's reflected in her main piece of advice:

'ALL THE ANSWERS THAT WE WANT ARE WITHIN US. LIVE YOUR OWN LIFE. WALK YOUR OWN PATH.'

— Dr Maki Mandela

SUPER MARIO TESTINO

ARIO TESTINO'S HQ IS EXACTLY what you would
hope the home of one of the world's most famous
photographers would be like. For a start, the outside
of the building is painted as fashionably black as a supermodel's
LBD. Then inside, it's all white and light; big, open studio spaces
that cry out for camera equipment and celebrities to turn up so
the maestro can do his work. Upon the walls rest shot after shot
of some of the world's most famous, beautiful and talented people,
all of whom have stared down Mario's lens and come out looking
all the better for it.

In the flesh, Mario is model-handsome himself and under-
statedly dressed in various shades of navy blue. He is charming
to talk to, but if you're prone to feelings of envy, then stay
away from his Instagram feed. It is an endless stream of photos
of fabulous people in wonderful places doing amazing things.
And it's not faked, that is actually what his life consists of. I
tell him he seems to be one of the few people whose life is
as good as it looks from the outside. He confirms my suspi-
cions. *'I work in a world of the most beautiful people, girls and
guys, travelling to the most beautiful places. And I am never anywhere*

in the world for more than five days. I am so lucky. But I really had to pay my dues to get here. I spent twelve years struggling to get work and start living, and now I work a minimum of twelve hours daily.'

Mario grew up in a big and loving family in Peru. He was a good student and everyone, including himself, assumed he was heading for a professional career in law or economics. However, when he hit his teenage years he *'started to dress weirdly: bright colours, stripes, dots, yellow with orange with blue, I couldn't help it, I had to wear the most outrageous things'*. His parents, while not understanding it, didn't stop him. But it became clear to all that he did not fit in with his conservative, Roman Catholic home country: *'people looked at me like I was a bit of a freak'*. After he tried three different university courses, and after six months of begging his parents, they sent him to London.

He loved Britain from the beginning. *'I found freedom in England, mental freedom, not physical freedom, people here are uptight with their bodies, but they're free with their minds, they can understand everything.'* He felt instinctively he could be himself. He applied to and was accepted by a London polytechnic to do communication studies. The programme did not start till the following year so Mario embarked on a course at a local photography school. Through a friend, Mario was introduced to an Iranian photographer who had just opened a photography studio and Mario was offered a non-paid job as her assistant. *'In a funny way I learnt more there than I did at the photography school and it taught me that was what I wanted to do.'*

From there he said he had no problem getting jobs immediately, but he lost them immediately too. *'I would convince and beg people to book me, but I would then light it all wrong and lose the job. It was all on film then, so you couldn't see your mistakes until it was too late.'* Over time the lessons were learnt, he started to keep some jobs and get rebooked for others, and he has been doing *Vogue* shoots now for over thirty years.

He says his enduring success has come down to his insistence on always trying to find the persona of the thing or person he is shooting. *'As a photographer, you have two options; it can either be about you or it can be about the person you're photographing. I don't do a picture of the Royals thinking of Mario Testino or a picture for Burberry thinking of Mario Testino, I create something for each of them, which captures them.'*

Given his global success at doing this, he is unpretentious about his work. *'What people forget is we are sales people, we make things look good. We can sell you a jacket, a dress, a car, a country, a family, we can sell you anything. We can make you want it.'*

He also credits his success to his personal credence of being continually open to change, to movement, to whatever is new. *'I always say I want to be nothing, because then I can be everything, I can be whatever I want to be. Sexuality, taste in food, music, colours, clothes. They all change. I've learnt you can never say you like red, because then it's black, then it's yellow, then it is green.'*

The biggest lesson he says he's learnt from his experiences is therefore to remain malleable, to not resist where life takes you.

'LIFE IS FUNNY. IT CAN BE SO RANDOM, SO YOU HAVE TO LEARN HOW TO SWAY. YOU HAVE TO BE OPEN TO WHAT SLIGHTLY PUZZLES YOU, TO WHAT YOU FEEL CURIOUS ABOUT, NOT JUST WHAT YOU ALREADY LIKE BECAUSE THEN THERE'S NO SPACE TO GROW AND

BECOME MORE. IN PERU
WHERE I GREW UP THERE
ARE EARTHQUAKES, AND THE
BUILDINGS THAT ARE BUILT
TO SWAY AND MOVE ARE THE
ONES THAT USUALLY SURVIVE.
THE ONES THAT ARE TOO
STIFF TEND TO CRACK AND
FALL DOWN.'

— *Mario Testino*

INSIDE THE WIRE WITH
LT COL LUCY GILES

As soon as I get out of the car I hear gunfire. It's a suitably authentic backing track for visiting Sandhurst, the military academy where every single officer in the British Army gets trained. Six hundred hopefuls undertake the course each year, hoping to pass out as an army officer, and every single one of them is the responsibility of Lieutenant Colonel Lucy Giles, the first female college commander in history to run this most revered of military institutions.

I'm not known for my punctuality, but given I'm meeting with someone who is used to commanding armies, I make an effort to get there early. Even so, Lucy is already waiting for me at the gatehouse, shoulders back, spine erect, cap down over the eyes. All the army personnel are referring to her as 'M'am'. I wonder if I ought to too.

Fortunately, she puts me at ease. She suggests we *'go have a brew'* and we plan a retreat through the grounds to her office in the main house. Other than the evil-looking assault course and the odd tank parked up at the side of the driveway, we could be within the confines of a beautiful stately home. In total, Sandhurst covers sixteen square kilometres and features unspoilt woodland, natural lakes, sweeping lawns and classic old buildings where the officers and Lucy are housed. And from the vantage point of Lt Col Giles's desk she can see the parade ground, where twenty-four years ago she herself was one of the trainee officers standing to attention.

Those twenty-four years have seen a big change in the way the army regards women. Yes, there was some sexism in the early years, inappropriate jokes about bikes and the usual nonsense, but Lucy maintains that that way of thinking has been relegated to history. The army today would simply not tolerate it, and it never got in the way of her soldiering, with Lucy having led operations and deployments in Bosnia, Iraq, Afghanistan, Sierra Leone and Northern Ireland.

In addition to the big job she fulfils now, she's also a mum of two and a wife to a soldier. *'It takes some juggling,'* she says, raising her eyebrows slightly, and the family home is *'inside the wire'*, the phrase for living within the perimeter of a military compound such as Sandhurst. In short, Lt Col Giles lives and breathes the army.

Her way into this world was due mainly to chance and curiosity. While at Exeter Uni a college friend suggested Lucy come along to an Officers' Training Corps weekend and Lucy fell in love with the whole experience: the physical and mental challenge, the social side, the sense of duty, the emphasis on development and people that is the army's modus operandi. It opened her up to opportunities and skills *('I even learnt how to use a fork to break into a Mini')* that this average student from a

Somerset comprehensive wouldn't otherwise have experienced. And here she is, a quarter of a century later, shaping the officer class of the entire institution.

I ask her how it feels. The response I get is a massive grin and a heartfelt *'I'm chuffed to bits.'* She relishes the role for the same reason she was originally drawn to the army: it is about getting the best from people. So what advice does she have for doing so?

She explains her approach as *'train in, rather than select out'*. It is about spotting the potential in people and giving them the opportunities to develop, rather than looking for people who are the finished article and getting rid of the rest. The training has a strong element of physicality and discipline, but just as much emphasis is put on softer skills such as decision-making, motivation and communication. As a soldier, you need to be able to deliver the tough stuff when necessary, but a lot of the role is about developing clear plans and communicating, capturing hearts and minds, not just bad guys.

Fundamentally, she says everything comes down to values. The army has a set – courage, discipline, respect for others, integrity, loyalty and selfless commitment. And her job is to make sure these are ingrained. They are what makes a soldier a British Army soldier.

'If you find yourself standing outside at night getting punished for having fluff on your jumper, it's because you didn't have, at a very small level, the discipline to check your kit before inspection. And if you extract that small issue to a different context – say you forget to put your safety catch on your weapon and it accidentally goes off and kills someone –

you can see why we do it. Everything we do is grounded in the purpose of us being better soldiers.'

She summarises her style of leadership as *'Drink more tea'*: get out from behind the desk and spend time with the troops, to have a brew and a chat to find out what's going on with them; be alongside them, both literally and figuratively, in the trenches. At Sandhurst she'll often get in full battle kit and go jog alongside the troops in training. She'll already have some intel on those who are struggling so she makes sure she runs alongside them, asks a few questions, works out what's up, sees if she can help: *'I'm quite Mother Hen-like in that regard.'*

Having values, living up to them and helping others do the same is what makes a great soldier. But Lucy sees it as exactly the same for life in general.

> **'Life for me is about doing the right thing, on a difficult day, when no one is looking. If you do something or walk by something that you know is not right, then you're ultimately cheating and undermining your own self. If you do the right thing, no matter what the outcome, your confidence always grows. And you have a better life that way. So just make sure you are always honest with yourself. And make sure you always do the right thing.'**

Yes, M'am.

'LIFE IS ABOUT DOING THE RIGHT THING, ON A DIFFICULT DAY, WHEN NO ONE IS LOOKING.'

– *Lt Col Lucy Giles*

ANTHONY BOURDAIN, LEAN, MEAN GRILLING MACHINE

I F YOU'VE EVER READ *Kitchen Confidential*, the restaurant petticoat-lifting book by Anthony Bourdain, bad-boy chef, writer and TV presenter, you'll already know his advice to never order fish on a Tuesday. Here are some additional pearls of wisdom he gave me recently, in his words. All I will say is, I'm very glad I got to our appointment early.

1. Turn the f**k up on time
'I am punctual, that's probably the most useful lesson I ever learned. It is the first evidence of your character I have: are you the sort of person who says they're going to do something and then doesn't? Being on time is the first thing I require of my cooks. If you have problems doing that, chances are I'm wasting my time showing you how to make hollandaise sauce. It's the same in social relationships, do you have enough respect for me to show up on time or do you not? If you don't, we're probably going to have problems down the line.'

2. Working in a kitchen will straighten you out
'I was a spoiled, narcissistic, lazy, self-involved middle-class kid from the

suburbs. *I'm a person who, left to my own natural instincts, will gravitate towards chaos and self-destruction and addiction. But working in a kitchen forced upon me a discipline that stopped me spinning out. I started as a dishwasher at seventeen, and, it may have taken thirty years, but I learnt how to grow up and be an adult there.'*

3. Be polite to waiters

'If you're mean or dismissive of waiters and hotel staff, you're dead to me, or if not dead to me you are bleeding out – our time together is going to be very limited. Because if you're pissy to waiters, that's the real you: you may not be like that to me now, but you will be.'

4. Don't work with assholes

'If you don't like the people you work with, you'll end up fucking miserable. Any accrued benefits are kind of worthless because your life will be shit. If you're dealing with assholes the whole time, you'll die of a heart attack. You know the people I'm talking about. The ones that when you see their caller ID you think, "Oh fuck, I don't want to talk to them." Well, don't do business with those people. Mickey Corleone said it isn't personal, it's business. Bullshit: all business is personal.'

5. When you're a cook, you can't bullshit anyone

'The kitchen is a world of absolutes: you either can or cannot cook 300 eggs Benedict in a three-hour shift. You might talk about how great you are all the time, but we're going to find out. Whatever you say before or afterwards is meaningless. But if you're really good, they'll bump you up. It's like the Mafia: if you kill eight people, you get to be a made guy.

6. If you get a lucky break, work it

'If you're forty-four years old like I was, and you've fucked up your life in every way like I had, make sure you recognise a lucky break when you get one, like I did with my book. Then work really hard at not fucking it up because that's what most people do when they get lucky. I managed to avoid that. I didn't have a plan, I just worked hard, avoided assholes and always turned up on time.'

7. Don't be a dick

'If I'm at your house and you offer me something to eat I don't particularly like, I'm going to smile and eat it. Try to be a good guest, try to be grateful, be a good guy, don't be a dick.'

8. Avoid hippies

'Hippies. I hate hippies and I hate their music. Bad for morale, bad work habits. And they are never on time.'

As I say, I'm glad I turned up early.

'IF YOU'RE FORTY-FOUR YEARS OLD LIKE I WAS, AND YOU'VE FUCKED UP YOUR LIFE IN EVERY WAY LIKE I HAD, MAKE SURE YOU RECOGNISE A LUCKY BREAK WHEN YOU GET ONE, LIKE I DID WITH MY BOOK. THEN WORK REALLY HARD AT NOT

FUCKING IT UP BECAUSE THAT'S
WHAT MOST PEOPLE DO
WHEN THEY GET LUCKY.
I MANAGED TO AVOID THAT. I
DIDN'T HAVE A PLAN, I JUST
WORKED HARD, AVOIDED
ASSHOLES AND ALWAYS
TURNED UP ON TIME.'

– Anthony Bourdain

DOING TIME WITH
ALEXANDER McLEAN

O
UR DRIVER PARKS UP ALONGSIDE a group of mud huts scattered around a clearing of baked, dry earth, turns off the ignition and announces that we're here. I say that this can't be the right place; there aren't any walls or fences. *'Why would there be fences?'* replies the driver, confused by my comment. *'There isn't anywhere for the prisoners to escape to.'*

I'm having my expectations of what it is to be incarcerated in Africa blown apart by a ten-jail tour of Uganda and Kenya with Alexander McLean, the founder of the African Prisons Project (APP). This is our first stop, a prison farm, officially in the middle of nowhere among the vast prairie lands of rural northern Uganda. It's taken five hours of driving down unpaved roads to get here. But still, no fences at all?

Alexander explains that not only are walls unnecessary but the local community prefer it this way because then they can use the prison well. That's when I clock the prison's water pump, and the orderly queue in front of it, consisting not just of inmates but young school children too, both groups in their respective uniforms, happily waiting their turn to draw from the well; a scene unimaginable in the Western world.

Later, as we walk around the grounds, a prisoner comes bounding up to us. He is speaking in a local dialect that I can't understand, but one thing is clear: he is *very* excited to see Alexander. The prison officer who is with us translates: *'He says that Alexander McLean saved his life. Alexander visited the prisoner on death row and helped him mount an appeal. When the date came, Alexander swapped his suit, shirt and tie for the prisoner's rags so he would look smart before the judge. The appeal worked, and the prisoner will be a free man in a matter of days.'*

I turn to Alexander to verify the story, and in his grave and modest manner he nods and says it is true. I ask him, out of interest, did he get his suit back? *'I don't believe I did. I am sure he will return it one day,'* is his measured, if somewhat optimistic, reply.

This small interchange captures both the essence of APP's work and Alexander's unconditional commitment to it. APP goes into prisons where there are little or no medical, educational or legal facilities and doesn't leave until there are health centres, libraries, teachers and lawyers in place. They've reduced mortality rates by a factor of ten in some jails, coached illiterate inmates through all the stages of education (in some cases prisoners have obtained law degrees and now help other inmates), and have got countless death sentences overturned. Game-changing does not cover it. Alexander is a founder and leader so committed to the mission that he's even prepared to, literally, lose the shirt off his back.

In fact, that's not even the best example of how all-in Alexander is with regard to his work; that story comes when we visit a maximum-security prison closer to town. The conditions are beyond challenging. I spend time in an open cell with 280 men who have to alternate sleeping and sitting because there is not enough room for all of them to lie down at the same time. Even tougher than that is the TB 'ward', a bare, dark concrete room given over to quarantining those men with the contagious disease. While myself and my friend stay back at the doorway, concerned for our health, Alexander walks straight in and over to the man who appears in the worst health, gets down on his hands and knees, and with a small cloth starts to mop the man's brow and tend to him. Without being overly dramatic, I think to myself, that is exactly what Jesus would do.

Alexander is a religious man. He first visited Africa as an eighteen-year-old when he volunteered at a hospice in Uganda. It was when working in the hospital he noticed that prisoners brought in were often left chained to the bed and not given treatment. He couldn't help think that if they were treated this badly in hospital, how much worse would it be in prison? So he talked his way into one and found out. Such were the appalling conditions, he found himself compelled to raise money to build a basic health centre and library. His work reduced the mortality rate from 144 to twelve in one year, and he's not stopped doing such work since.

Alexander points out that most people in these prisons are there for crimes of poverty: stealing food, not paying debts, being a vagabond (the Dickensian-sounding 'crime' of being homeless). Most have not even been to trial; they are just held on remand.

The Ugandan constitution says that no one should wait more than six months for their day in court: the current average is two and a half years. The result: prisons are hugely overcrowded with, more often than not, innocent people. It's a depressing situation.

Alexander's work brings hope to such places. He of course makes no distinctions between whether people are innocent or not: he starts from the position that they are all human beings and deserve to be able to live and, inevitably sometimes, die with dignity. But more than that, he is motivated to tackle the lost opportunity of keeping people in captivity with no chance for change. He wants whatever time people have to spend in prison to be an opportunity for transformation, not despair. And I meet enough ex-death row prisoners-turned-lawyers assisting fellow inmates and recently trained prisoner-teachers leading English classes for other convicts to know such transformations are possible.

He is a truly remarkable man, shining light into some of the darkest places imaginable. His life is a manifestation of the advice he gives:

'The lowliest-looking person is filled with gifts and talents beyond your imagination. Love such people as yourself. Those living on the margins of society do not need to have their problems solved for them, they just need to be given the opportunities to solve them themselves. And in doing so, they will often also solve the problems of others.'

'THE LOWLIEST-LOOKING
PERSON IS FILLED WITH GIFTS
AND TALENTS BEYOND YOUR
IMAGINATION. LOVE SUCH
PEOPLE AS YOURSELF.'

— *Alexander McLean*

EDNA O'BRIEN,
CHAMPION OF THE WORD

AMONG THE GENTEEL, WEDDING-CAKE-COLOURED streets of Kensington, ending a terrace of rather prim and austere town houses, rests a smaller, simpler-looking cottage, a friendly country-cousin visiting its richer relations in the city. That cottage is the warm and slightly worn home of Edna O'Brien, the fiercely talented, proudly Irish writer of tectonic-plate-shifting *Country Girls* (and more than twenty other books since), and the person described by Philip Roth as 'the most gifted woman now writing in English'.

When I visit Edna, it's three days before the fateful Brexit referendum. Sat in her front room surrounded by the paper tools of her trade, we share our concern over the Vote Leave campaign, where half-truths and smears have been used to demean experts and divide the country.

Edna sees many of these tactics as examples of a wider, longer-term issue. '*There seems to be a notion that the louder you talk and the more obscene or semi-obscene words you can draw into the script, the more effective it is. There is a prevailing savagery and cruelty in the world that frightens me.*' It is something she has unfortunately been on the receiving end of herself. *Country Girls*, her first novel, was burned and banned in Ireland, and originally led to her being cast as a national hate figure, simply for writing (beautifully) about the sexual awakening of young Irish women. She is now revered as the country's greatest writer.

Her prescribed solution for reducing this ever-present, ever-rising vitriol is for us all to spend more time actually thinking and reflecting, rather than just adopting what we hear without due consideration and failing to be aware of ourselves in what we say and do. *'Much of our lives, with our rabbity brains, we are on automatic. We are restless and have lost our reflectiveness and concentration.'* To get it back, we need to read more, and preferably great literature. *'It is not elitist, it is not boring, reading deepens and quickens the native intelligence. I never went to university but I read or reread something very great every day and consider it part of my training, like a boxer has to punch every day.'*

Her training has paid off. Now in her mid-eighties, she is an undisputed international literary heavyweight champion of the word. Her most recent book, *The Little Red Chairs*, received the best reviews of her career, proof indeed that if you keep sharpening the sword it need not dull. But such quality does not come easily. *'I'm totally precise and obsessive about detail, I have to be, I couldn't write the way I do if I was more easy-going.'* And it can be a lonely life. *'If you were to ask me, which is better, having a companion or living alone? I would say the aloneness furthers the work, but it accumulates the sadness. There is no one to leave a tray outside my door while I write.'*

It's not a complaint. A woman of her intellect, charisma and beauty has had many offers, she's been married in the past so knows that life, and she is mother to two children whom she adores. Writing is what she has wanted to do since she was a young woman, and if she had to choose between her literary life or a life of domestic bliss, the books would win. But she does rather wonderfully confess, *'What I would like is a part-time husband or companion, so if you know anyone suitable for that challenge, tell him to head this way.'*

She is a woman who emotes passion; as we talk, strong feelings and determined opinions abound. She is also wildly funny. She warns of the constant clamour of social media − *'I would no more engage in tweeting than I would jump out that window'* − chastises the business elite for their *'gluttony for not just money but more money'*, and even tells me to *'talk less now'* when she has further views to impart. She is gloriously, defiantly alive, the deeper benefit that comes from a life fulfilling her childhood ambition to become a great writer.

It is therefore appropriate that her advice is an ode to a life spent in pursuit of what you dared dream for when you were younger.

'For each person who aspires to anything, retain the innocence and conviction of when you started out. Be open to the surprise and wonder and terror of the world, but remain faithful to your first aspiration. Never forget what bestirs you.'

EDNA O'BRIEN

❖

149

'Never forget what

bestirs you.'

— Edna O'Brien

THE INDEFINABLE NITIN
SAWHNEY

W HETHER YOU'RE LOOKING FOR AN internationally
acclaimed flamenco guitarist, a classical composer
for your new Hollywood movie score, a concert-
grade pianist to play the Albert Hall, an actor for your latest BBC
sit-com, a songwriter for Shakira's next track, or a big-beats DJ
to play the main room at Fabric, better call Nitin. Somewhat
amazingly, Nitin Sawhney, the writer/producer/musician/
composer/whatever does all of the above and more. And that's
just his musical side. If you've got a tough mathematical problem
you need solving, a legal issue to resolve, or some question over
this year's accounts, as a trained mathematician, lawyer and
accountant, he can help with all that too. Talented does not begin
to cover it.

I'm in his studio complex, an old dairy round the back of
Brixton high street. To get there, I've just walked past the shrine
to David Bowie, who recently passed away. The written outpour-
ings of grief and the sheer number of people who have made
the pilgrimage to it remind me of the simple fact that to a lot
of people music is life, or certainly one of the best parts of it.

Nitin Sawhney would agree. He describes the day when as a young boy a battered old piano turned up at home as *'one of the happiest moments of my life. I couldn't keep away from it. Banging the keys felt like an explosion of possibility. I could hear so many colours, there was so much potential for expression.'*

From a young age, he had a lot to say.

The background to this is Nitin's childhood in 1970s Rochester, Kent, which back then was a heartland of the National Front. Racism was rife and Nitin was the only Asian kid in his year, if not the whole school. There was *'a lot of violence towards me, a lot of racism, I had a terrible time and always felt like an outsider, but it gave me lots to think about. I had a need to get stuff out.'* With that piano, and music generally, he found a way of doing so.

Another, more positive influence from his childhood that helps explain his myriad approach to music came from his mum, an Indian classical dancer who took inspiration from all different art forms and types of music. She showed him that the boundaries people erect between different disciplines of art were imaginary, that all of music and art was pure expression and that it didn't need to be categorised.

To a certain extent, Nitin has fought the world's insecure need to categorise his work throughout his whole career. After being nominated for the Mercury Prize, he remembers being in a record shop and the display dedicated to that year's nominees featuring all eleven artists except him. When he asked why, he was told, *'Nitin Sawhney makes world music, so it's only sold out of that section.'* On a separate occasion when asked by a persistent journalist how he felt to be *'the leader of the Asian Underground'*, Nitin said he didn't understand the question. When the journalist kept asking the same thing, he says, *'I explained to him that I just made music; that it was neither Asian nor Underground, whatever that meant, and that I wasn't the leader of anything.'* The journalist ended the interview and wrote a piece labelling Nitin as deliberately obnoxious.

Nitin's philosophy and advice relate to some of these experiences and guide people to resist society's urge to label and categorise:

> *'Do not let others define you and your life. Do not be defined by other people's expectations of you. Do not be defined by time, either by what you've done up to this point, as that is the past, or by your ambitions, as that is the future. Tune into yourself and define yourself by being your authentic true self in every given moment. Find out what things feel good for your soul and do that. That's your freedom that you have. And it gives you the ballast to resist a world that's trying to manipulate or categorise you in some way.'*

Nitin Sawhney: indefinable.

THE ESSENCE OF JO MALONE

I T'S THE WEATHER OF UNICORNS – a sunny day in London – so we order rosé wine to celebrate. A selection is available, and the different wines are presented to sample. Jo Malone lifts each glass to try. I assume she's going to taste them, but she chooses simply by smelling each one. I think to myself afterwards, of course she does.

Jo Malone is one of the most famous fragrance-makers in the world. As the founder of not one but now two internationally successful perfume businesses, most people know the name but few know her story. If she were to capture the essence of that story in just three words it would be this: *'lemonade from lemons'*.

Jo is a self-described dyslexic working-class girl from Bexleyheath who's done good. She may have a natural-born talent for creating fragrances, which she partly credits to her dyslexia – *'My brain just works differently, I see textures and colours and can translate them back into smells and fragrances'* – but her first foray into beauty products was for traumatic reasons. When Jo was eleven, her mum had a serious nervous breakdown and social services said that if her mother was hospitalised Jo and her sister would have to go into care.

Amazingly, Jo convinced the social worker that she could handle the responsibility of providing for the family. To earn money, she recalled what she'd seen her mum do as a Revlon lady: make face creams at home and sell them to well-to-do ladies in Fulham. So she did that. It worked, making her enough money to look after the family until her mum recovered. '*I learnt early that when bad things happen you can either let them beat you or you can stand and fight. And if you do, you can always turn things round.*'

A second, earlier childhood experience proved equally formative: the time Jo was made to stand on a desk by a teacher as punishment for sneaking a look at a friend's exam paper (Jo's dyslexia meant she did not understand one of the written questions). '*I felt so utterly humiliated. And she said in front of the whole class that if you cheat you will never make anything of your life, Jo Malone.*'

When Jo recounts this story, you can still feel the emotional charge, even though it is nearly forty years later. '*I've remembered that moment all through my life. I've never allowed it to make me bitter, but I have allowed it to motivate me. I remember looking out of the window of our little house and thinking, "She's wrong. I'm going to make something of my life, I'm not going to stay here."*'

Of course, her childhood didn't consist of just these negative moments. She has fond memories of her dad: '*He was a brilliant human being but didn't know how to hold a family together.*' His life instead revolved around three things, all of which came to be instrumental in Jo's success: he was an artist, a market-trader and a magician, and Jo worked alongside him on all three. '*Saturday mornings I would work with him on the market, helping him sell his paintings, and in the evenings I was his magician's assistant. I had a pet white dove called Suki that my dad would make appear out of a pan of fire.'* Collectively these experiences schooled her in the tricks of the retailing trade, teaching her how to use stories and a bit of magic to captivate people, all crucial ingredients in the kaleidoscopic world of senses and surprises that she has created.

This blend of different experiences, both good and bad, have all contributed to Jo's life view. *'Looking back, everything was relevant. Nothing in life is wasted. You can make something positive from anything.'*

Being diagnosed with breast cancer in her mid-thirties was the ultimate test of this approach to life. She was dressed in her best suit and earrings on her way to a glamorous summer party when she got the news. Her doctor said it was one of the worst forms of aggressive breast cancer he'd seen and she had nine months left to live. Her instinct to fight did not kick in immediately. That came a bit later, as she sat on her bed crying, with her two-year-old son asking his mummy what the matter was.

'At the thought of leaving him, the spirit to fight just filled me. I thought to myself, "No one's going to tell me when I'm going to die. I'll tell you when I'm going to die."'

She credits her husband with a powerful piece of advice. *'He told me to fight the cancer in the same way I built my business, and that stuck in my mind. I knew that if I were in trouble in business, I would find the best lawyer. So I went to find the best doctor.'* Three days later Jo was on a plane to the US. She put herself in the care of a cutting-edge oncologist and endured chemotherapy every five days for a year, an unbelievably gruelling twelve months, but one that ultimately delivered the all-clear. *'On my last day of*

chemo I dressed in the same suit and earrings I was meant to go to that
party in, and I took back that day that the cancer took from me.'

While beating cancer is clearly the biggest obstacle she has had
to overcome, Jo talks about selling her business as being traumatic
too. Not only did she suffer that sense of loss entrepreneurs often
feel when they exit their company, she also lost the right to use
her own name in the future, as that was now owned by the new
company, and she no longer got to do the thing she loved most
in the world: make fragrances. So what did she do? As soon as
her non-compete contract ended, she started building her second
empire, Jo Loves, one scent and one shop at a time.

Her advice reflects this lifelong spirit of defiance and refusal
to be dictated to by external circumstances. She counsels that we
should remember that, ultimately, we are always in control.

> **'No matter how bad it is, no situation is ever greater than**
> **you. You always have three options: you can change the**
> **situation, accept the situation or change your mindset on**
> **how you see the situation. And you have the power in your**
> **hands to choose whichever is best for you. Never allow**
> **something else or someone's opinion to become the title of**
> **your book. Ever.'**

She says the last part with such verve and passion it's clear that
if you could take what Jo's got and bottle it, you'd make a lot of
money.

'I LEARNT EARLY THAT WHEN BAD THINGS HAPPEN YOU CAN EITHER LET THEM BEAT YOU OR YOU CAN STAND AND FIGHT. AND IF YOU DO, YOU CAN ALWAYS TURN THINGS ROUND.'

– Jo Malone

BEAR GRYLLS, BORN SURVIVOR

YOU COULD BE FORGIVEN FOR assuming that Bear Grylls, ex-soldier, Everest climber, world-renowned survival expert and adventurer, would be a bit macho, hardened by his time as a soldier and his many brushes with death – but not so. I wouldn't be so stupid as to call Bear a bit of a softy, especially when sat right in front of him, but he has a warmth and gentleness you don't necessarily expect of your typical SAS commando.

We're chatting backstage after Bear has just talked to hundreds of teachers about tackling Everest at a young age (he reached the summit at twenty-three, two years after a sky-diving accident in which he fractured his spine and was told he may never walk again) and the source of his drive and resilience. Interestingly, when you hear him recount his adventures, there's no bravado: achievements are downplayed, credit for them is assigned to others, and he portrays himself as someone who constantly struggles along the way.

In Bear's world struggling is OK. In fact, it is enduring the struggle that leads to the success.

'There's always going to be someone faster, smarter, taller, more *experienced than you, but the rewards in life don't always go to them, the rewards in life go to the dogged, the determined, those who can keep going and pick themselves back up and never say die and just hang in there, sometimes quietly and undramatically.'*

One-on-one, his humbleness remains and, while not shy, he comes across as someone more comfortable heading up a mountain than to a cocktail party. First and foremost, he's a family man. Much of what he says relates back either to his parents or his experience of being one himself. His introduction to the world of adventure came from his dad, who took him climbing when he was young. Bear loved the bonding experience, with his father quite literally showing him the ropes. *'It was the first time I found something I was good at. I never did well at school, but I could climb higher than anyone else.'* It opened him up to a life of *'being outdoors, going on adventures, getting muddy, and doing a job I couldn't even have dreamt of back as a young boy'.*

As with most people who have a career that professionalises a relationship with danger, he's extremely respectful of the risks he takes. He makes it clear that he didn't 'conquer' Everest: *'we didn't conquer anything, we made it to the top by the skin of our teeth and got away with our lives where others hadn't'.* Four people he knew died on the mountain at the same time Bear was climbing it.

He lightens the mood by recounting the time he proudly showed his mum the photo of himself at the summit of Everest, a picture taken after a gruelling three-month expedition, with days spent in the death zone gasping for air, knowing each footstep could be his last. She took one look at the shot and said, *'Oh, Bear, it would have been so much nicer if you could have just combed your hair.'*

'*Mums will be mums,*' he says, smiling at the memory.

He accredits part of his ability to endure the hardships of his adventuring to his faith. While he points out '*there are no atheists in the death zone*', his quiet Christianity is something he calls upon away from the mountains on a daily basis. '*I know I can't depend just on self-confidence, by myself I am not strong enough, but developing a confidence in something much stronger than me gives me more power, so I start every day on my knees just quietly asking for help and wisdom and to say sorry for the things I got wrong yesterday.*'

He's non-evangelical about his faith but open about it and, it has to be said, gives God some great PR opportunities. When one of his all-time heroes, President Obama, came on his *Running Wild* show to raise awareness of climate change, as well as schooling Mr President on the dangers of fornicating bears and the benefits of drinking urine, he also asked if he could pray with the President, who, as another man of faith and family values, readily agreed.

Given his approach to faith, family and friendships, it's surprising that Bear is sometimes the target of criticism for his TV shows, which some claim promote machismo and the spilling of blood and sweat and tears. He has no time for that negativity and says anyone who thinks that's the take-away from his programmes is missing the point. In fact, he says what his TV programmes show, time and time again, is what he also puts forward as his best piece of advice*:*

'IT IS NOT THE MOST
MASCULINE, MACHO, OR THE
ONES WITH THE BIGGEST
MUSCLES WHO WIN. IT'S
THOSE WHO LOOK AFTER
EACH OTHER, WHO REMAIN
CHEERFUL IN ADVERSITY, WHO
ARE KIND AND PERSISTENT AND
POSITIVE. THESE ARE THE
CHARACTERISTICS THAT HELP
YOU, NOT JUST TO SURVIVE

LIFE BUT TO ENJOY IT. AND
THEY'RE NOTHING TO DO
WITH GENDER. THE PEOPLE
WHO ARE SUCCESSFUL ARE THE
ORDINARY ONES THAT JUST
GO THAT LITTLE BIT FURTHER,
WHO GIVE A LITTLE MORE
THAN THEY ARE ASKED TO,
WHO LIVE WITHIN THAT
EXTRA FIVE PER CENT.'

– *Bear Grylls*

THE EDUCATION OF DAMBISA
MOYO

F YOU EVER WANT A role model for the transformational power of education and the unlimited potential of Africa, you will struggle to find a better candidate than the global economist and best-selling author Dambisa Moyo. Born and raised in post-colonial Zambia, forty years later she's sitting before me as an Oxford PhD- and Harvard MBA-wielding, Barclays board-sitting, *Time Magazine* 100 Most Influential People in the World-ranking, razor-sharp woman with enough energy to power her home continent.

She is crystal clear on how she made the journey from her origins to the life she leads now. *'The linchpin of my life was being able to go to school.'* She sets this in context: *'Look, I've got no birth certificate, because at the time of my birth, birth certificates were not issued to blacks, so you can imagine there wasn't much emphasis on girls like me going to school.'* But her parents were different. Even though they had been born into a country where there were restrictions on blacks going to school, they knew the importance of Dambisa getting an education. *'They said, "You have to go to school, we don't know what that might look like for you, but you've got to go and do that." And that changed the trajectory of my life forever.'*

Her African schooling is something she is grateful for and why she rallies against, and works to overturn, the lazy misconceptions of Africa as a hopeless cause, dependent on aid. *'Alongside the Caribbean Islands, my continent produces over 90 per cent of the blacks that go to the Ivy League universities in the United States. Africa is viewed as the continent of corruption and disease, poverty and war, but it's the source of the vast majority of blacks that go to those schools and can compete globally. As a child, I was better educated in Africa than many people I know who grew up in the West.'*

She fears that these same Western societies are becoming inadvertently racially disconnected, where blacks and whites live in the same cities but with increasingly separate lives. *'I just came from a business lunch in Mayfair. There were sixty people there. I was the only black person and the only woman. I knew people there, and I would go to the gallows saying they are not racist. But I looked around and thought "Wow, this is 2016 and this is London and, if I weren't here, there wouldn't be a single black person or woman in this room."'*

She is also clear that direct forms of prejudice are still alive and well in the twenty-first century. She tells the quietly shocking story of attending her first public AGM/shareholders' meeting of a large global company as their newly appointed director. Sitting on stage alongside her fellow twelve board colleagues – who all happened to be white and male – one question from the floor was a woman crossly asking, *'I want to know what credentials that woman has to allow her to be on the board.'* When the chairman explained that all his board members were of the highest calibre, the lady got agitated, saying you have to answer my question, what are *her* credentials. A colleague of hers was quick to point out, *'She has a Doctorate in Economics from Oxford, a Masters from Harvard and worked for ten years at Goldman Sachs. Is there anything else you want to say?'*

I asked Dambisa if the assumption that she doesn't deserve to be there rails her in some way. *'It's what you deal with every single day being a minority. You learn to not respond to it and to not let it define you. So I just sat there and thought, "Look, lady, I'm fine, you don't need to worry about me and my credentials." And here's the thing, when I walked off the podium, two of the male board members said to me, "Thank God they didn't ask about my credentials," including one who said he hadn't even been to college.'*

When it comes to her most valuable advice, it is these decades of confounding expectations and enduring ignorant assumptions about Africa, about women, about her colour that serve as the backdrop to a deeper, more fundamental piece of guidance:

> *'I know it sounds kind of corny, but every day I look in the mirror and I tell myself that I am going to go out there and face it and not curl up in a ball because somebody said something or thinks that I couldn't be or do something simply because of who I am. It's hard, but you have to do it. Put in the hard work, discipline and focus and just keep going. Remember there are numerous people, both similar and dissimilar to you, who are rooting for you to stay strong, and to prove the naysayers wrong.'*

THE BEAT OF MICKEY HART

R EMARKABLE PEOPLE TEND TO BE focused; it tends to
go with the territory. But no one, and I do mean no
one, is more focused than Mickey Hart, drummer of
the Grateful Dead, the seminal psychedelic rock band from the
1960s to the present day. Mickey's 'thing' is rhythm. And he is all
in.

On the occasion our paths first cross, I hear him before I see
him. There's a beat – a knocking, tocking sound – and a haunting
wail coming from a secluded, fire-lit corner in this remote part
of the Guatemalan Highlands where we're staying.

Intrigued, I move towards the beat and find Mickey, cross-
legged on the floor, eyes closed, gently swaying in front of the
fire, with four Mayan shamans blowing, shaking and hitting their
traditional ceremonial instruments, the same ancient rhythms and
noises the Mayans have been making among these rainforest-clad
hills for millennia. And Mickey is *feeling* it.

He's flown into this far-flung spot to jam with the shamans
in his never-ending search for new sounds and beats. This is what
he does. He does rhythm.

To put this into context, this is a man who has a specially built lab at home in which he sits wearing his own specially built rhythm helmet, a device wired up to an MRI scanner to measure the effect on his brain of the different beats he plays. This is the same man who has worked with NASA to listen to the rhythm of the universe, recording the distant beats and rumbles from remote galaxies, describing the Big Bang as *'the first note, the downbeat of the universe'*. It's all pretty cosmic, in every sense of the word, but these are serious endeavours. His latest project has him working with doctors on a study of the effect of different rhythms on disease: are there certain frequencies that can affect unhealthy cells and help them? If anyone can find out, it's Mickey.

His advice, therefore, came as no surprise.

> *'If I was to give one piece of advice, it is this: life is all about rhythm. Your heartbeat, great sex, the seasons, how often you call your parents, your good days versus your bad days, your DNA, the universe: everything has a rhythm. You have to develop a well-stretched ear and listen. The more you listen for the rhythm of your life, the more you will hear it. Find your rhythm. Live your life to its beat.'*

But for now he is back with the shamans. They're still playing in their trance-like state, summoning past ancestors, gods and monsters. Mickey is reverential to the shamans and respectful of their traditions, but he's also a perfectionist. To his ear, something's not quite right, something's a little off. It's the conch shell. Or more specifically it is the way the conch shell is being blown. Mickey knows a better way. He stops the proceedings, explains via the translator the nature of the issue, and in one short blast Mickey improves on 5,000 years of technique. The shamans look impressed.

'FIND YOUR RHYTHM.
LIVE YOUR LIFE TO ITS BEAT.'

— Mickey Hart

HAVING WORDS
WITH CLARE BALDING

I THINK I'VE JUST BEEN CALLED a 'beta male'. I'm with Clare Balding and we're talking about gender equality and she said that the growth of the beta male is a positive thing, and looked approvingly at me. I'm not quite sure how I feel about being seen as one. I think I may secretly like it, which, if so, basically proves her assertion. And presumably makes her alpha female, at least in this conversation.

Certainly when it comes to presenting Clare Balding takes first place, no contest. She's been in front of the camera at six Olympic Games, five Paralympics, three Winter Olympics, two Wimbledons, countless horse-racing events and a never-ending stream of TV shows and radio programmes. Add to that a best-selling memoir, constant public speaking and a new kids' book, and you get the sense of an ambitious woman who works as hard as the athletes she interviews.

When the word 'ambition' comes up, it gives rise to a moment of reflection. *'It's funny, I have had so many old-fashioned newspaper critics write, "She's very ambitious", as if it's negative because I am a woman. But I think, "Too bloody right I'm ambitious, why shouldn't I be? Should I want to come second?"'*

Sexism is unfortunately nothing new to Clare. She's been exposed to it since the day she was born, quite literally. *'My grandmother took one look at me in the crib and said to my father, "Oh, it's a girl. Never mind, you'll just have to keep on trying."'* That set the tone for a family life in which Clare was constantly told women can't do certain things and should behave in a certain way. Fortunately, it had the opposite effect and she's been proving them wrong ever since.

A background radiation of homophobia is another thing she has had to grow used to. *'A lot of people throw stones at me on social media and a lot of those stones are labelled "dyke".'* It took her seven years to come out to her parents, because *'I was so concerned about the shame of it, but I eventually woke up to the fact that I was complicit in the shame.'* Her advice to anyone in the closet is to get out of it damn quick. *'You're not protecting yourself and you're not protecting others, you are in fact protecting the prejudice. Be proud, not ashamed.'* And she is optimistic that the world is becoming increasingly accepting of the LGBT community, recounting a sweet conversation she had recently with her five-year-old niece. *'She said to me, "You're married, aren't you, Aunty Clare?" I said, "Yes, I am," and she said, "So girls can marry girls and boys can marry boys?" I said, "Yes, they can." And she said, "Well, that's good, isn't it?" So for this generation it will always have been normal.'*

As well as the ambition and optimism, you also get the sense of a woman who is perpetually interested. It is in fact one of the main pieces of advice she passes on: *'everything you do is an opportunity to learn, every person has a story to tell, if you think someone is dull it is because you're asking the wrong questions'*. With a natural curiosity, she has found her true vocation in a career that involves researching, interviewing, presenting.

She takes the gig seriously, and is rightly respected for having won every gong that's going for presenting. In her view, it's about helping the viewer experience at home what she is experiencing being right there in the middle of the action. *'It is almost creating a virtual reality but without the glasses.'* To be able to do so, according to Clare, you have to remove all ego: it is never about the presenter, but about what is going on around you. The other critical thing is vocabulary. You need to build evocative sentences easily and quickly. Her trick for that is to read a lot of literature, especially poetry, so she has the language to hand to bring what she's seeing to life in words.

Maybe it is a coincidence, but her most valuable piece of advice is about words, in this case specifically adjectives:

> *'In life, we are not what we look like, we are not our gender, sexuality or religion or race, we are how we act and the impact that we have on others. And the best way to think about the impact we have on others is in adjectives. I ask myself "What person do I want to be?" But in adjectives, not nouns. How about kind? Healthy? Ambitious? Does thinking like that get me to a more fruitful and satisfying place? I think it probably does.'*

It's an original way of thinking about personal growth and leaves me with just one question: is 'beta' an adjective?

'I've had old-fashioned newspaper critics write, "She's very ambitious", as if it's negative because I am a woman. But I think, "Too bloody right I'm ambitious, why shouldn't I be? Should I want to come second?"'

– *Clare Balding*

NANCY HOLLANDER,
JIU-JITSU LAWYER

I'M SITTING DRINKING PEPPERMINT TEA with David, Goliath's nemesis. But David is not how I expected him to be. Firstly, he is a woman. Secondly, she's American. And finally, she's petite and seventy-two.

You have probably not heard of Nancy Hollander, which is a good thing for you personally. As an American criminal defence and civil rights attorney, you'd only come across her if you were, rightly or wrongly, in trouble. But without her, there is a dark part of the world we would know a lot less about: Guantánamo Bay.

Nancy Hollander is the lawyer of two of the men incarcerated in that prison, set up on foreign land by the US government under the Bush administration. It did so, seemingly, with the deliberate aim not to just imprison men they suspected of terrorist activity, but to do so indefinitely, unaccountably, with no charge but with plenty of torture, and in direct contravention of constitutional and human rights. However, if Nancy knows one thing, it is that the law is bigger than the government. So she is fourteen years into a legal fight on behalf of her clients to get the

US government to abide by its own laws. It is a painfully slow battle but one she is starting to win.

As a master strategist, she engineered a tactical success by winning the right for one of her clients, Mohamedou Ould Slahi, to publish his *Guantánamo Diary*, a memoir recounting the extraordinary rendition, dark sites, savage beatings, torture and sexual humiliation he has experienced during his fourteen years in captivity. It made uncomfortable reading, especially for the American government. The furore around the book helped to bring attention not just to the abuses but also to the reality of Mohamedou's situation, that he had been held in Guantánamo Bay for well over a decade, uncharged with any crime, and even after the former chief prosecutor in Guantánamo had said publicly there was no evidence that Mohamedou ever committed any violence against the United States.

His case, or lack of one, has been a troubling manifestation of the illegal practices that Nancy constantly fights.

But in this case she has fought successfully: after nearly a decade, and as this book goes to print, she has just obtained approval for his release, although an actual date is still to be given. Her work continues.

In conversation, Nancy is absolutely focused on due process. She will not reveal a single piece of potentially classified information about any of her clients or the conditions in which they are held, even if that information is already in the public sphere. She will not do anything that could potentially give the US government opportunity to undermine her or her achievements to date. Her one action outside formal procedure is the metal kangaroo badge permanently pinned to her lapel, a silent protest of the 'kangaroo court' style of justice her clients are being subjected to.

As a young woman growing up in Texas in the 1950s, she was no stranger to injustice. Aged ten, she was the only student in a class debate to support the Brown vs Board of Education court case that said segregated public schools were unconstitutional. Her teachers rang her parents to say they were worried about her for being so strident. But as *'intellectual lefties'* they supported her. At age seventeen she would follow police paddy wagons around Chicago at night, taking photos of cops beating up people. She has been arrested on three separate occasions for peaceful protest and has spent her entire life fighting for people's rights, irrespective of what they may or may not have done. She may be a small woman, but she stands tall and resolute in front of power.

What comes out in our conversation is that Nancy is an avid practitioner of martial arts, and jiu-jitsu in particular, and she uses the principles taught by her sensai in taking on opponents much bigger than herself:

> ***'Whatever you do, do it with intent. In martial arts we call it "one plus one". Just one good kick and one good punch is better than twenty you didn't have any intent behind. Do not say something unless you mean it, do not do something unless you are committed. Do not confront by shouting, but confront by using your intellectual powers and the power of a better argument, by standing your***

ground, by keeping your centre, by never transgressing so they cannot attack. Ultimately, the trick is to absorb and redirect their energy. You use their own power against themselves.'

None of this is at small cost to herself. Her tireless work has meant she's been accused of being a terrorist sympathiser or a flat-out terrorist, purely for her insistence that the government follows its own constitution and prosecutes people fairly. She says that the people who have criticised her the most savagely have been those within, or connected to, the Bush administration. Which she says is ironic, as they are the ones who, by falsifying reports, condoning torture and signing off on extraordinary renditions, have been breaking the law. And who, therefore, one day may need her services most.

Absorb and redirect indeed.

'Whatever you do, do it with intent. Just one good kick and one good punch is better than twenty you didn't have any intent behind. Do not say something unless you mean it, do not do something unless you are committed.'

— *Nancy Hollander*

JUDE'S LAW

O N THE DAY WE MEET, time is running out for Jude Law. Not in respect to life generally, but on his parking meter. To avoid the faff of finding loose change and re-parking, we decide to sit and talk in his car, pulled up on the side of Shaftesbury Avenue, a kind of poor man's *Carpool Karaoke*.

We chat about our respective childhoods. I mention I grew up in Huddersfield, and to my surprise Jude says he's going there at the weekend. No disrespect to my hometown, but it's not normally a place where international movie stars go to hang out. When I enquire what takes him there, he explains it is to meet with the uncle of a young Syrian boy who Jude befriended when he visited The Jungle, the makeshift refugee camp in Calais. The child-refugee in question had seen his mum, dad and siblings die in the crossing from Africa and was in the camp all alone, so Jude offered to pay the legal fees and oversee the process of getting him out of the camp and into the arms of his one remaining family member up in Huddersfield.

The fact that Jude went several times to the refugee camp in the first place, is doing all this personally for the young lad, and, most tellingly, it only comes up in conversation because of an unlikely coincidence says a lot about the guy off screen.

In fact, Jude Law has a long history of going the extra mile to support important causes. On previous occasions he travelled to the Democratic Republic of the Congo and to Afghanistan with the peace-making organisation Peace One Day; he was part of an initiative that managed to broker a twenty-four-hour cease-fire agreement between the Taliban and the American military in Afghanistan, the result being that during the brief cessation 10,000 health workers were mobilised and inoculated 1.4 million children.

He puts his track record of stepping out of the limelight and into pretty tough places down to several things. One is to make sense of this strange thing called fame. *'I'm in no way comparing myself to him, but my hero John Lennon said, "If you're going to poke a camera in my face, then I am going to say something important." That's the worth of media and fame, to help important things get noticed.'* He also says if he were to stick to just the movie-star life of five-star hotels and VIP experiences then he would *'feel fat with guilt'*. On the most basic level he has a curiosity about the world and a desire to engage with as many different aspects of it as possible. His perspective is essentially, *'Why wouldn't you want to go to these places?'*

This ethos of experiencing life for its own sake is echoed in his advice for people who want to make it as an actor. *'There is such a large amount of luck needed to get your moment, so you have to be in acting for the right reasons: do it because you love the thing, the process, because you'll enjoy doing a no-pay play in a room above a pub.*

You have to be happy doing it that way, because what happens otherwise if you don't get your break?' He says it is having that love of the actual thing that will keep you sane if you do make it because otherwise *'it can fast start to feel like a business and you will need to keep that original flame alight or you can lose your way'*.

When I ask for his single best piece of wisdom, we revert back to talking about his childhood, and he credits his dad with his favourite piece of advice, given to him as a young boy:

'If you are going to be late, enjoy being late.'

It was a piece of advice he meant literally: that if you are late, rather than panic and get stressed, enjoy the extra time it is affording you. But as a piece of advice it has served Jude as a wider metaphor for life, reminding him to *'relish the moment, be in the moment, do the right thing in the moment, whatever that moment is'*, be it in a refugee camp, a room above a pub or the set of your latest blockbuster.

And with that, he has to go. He's running late.

'If you are
late, enjoy

*going to be
being late.'*

– JUDE LAW

PILLOW TALK
WITH JOAN BAKEWELL

AGED EIGHTY-THREE, JOAN BAKEWELL, THE much-loved BBC presenter, writer and member of the House of Lords, is a woman who has no time for getting old. Not only is she too busy to pay it any regard, she simply rejects the whole concept of it in the first place. *'I don't believe in the so-called declining years. Every day is a full twenty-four hours, with sixty minutes in each hour, and it is the same amount of time whether you are twelve, twenty, forty or eighty. You're getting as much daylight as anyone else and the same amount you've ever got. It's up to you what you do with it.'*

We're having this conversation in her bookish town house set in the corner of a leafy North London square. And when I say bookish, I mean it literally. Books really are everywhere. *'I know, I've got so many of the damn things.'* She tells me she has a solution. Every Saturday and Sunday she has started putting a box outside her house of the books she's read and passers-by help themselves. It's a solution that neatly matches her career of spreading ideas and putting things out there.

In conversation, Joan comes across as a woman with her yin and yang right where she wants them. She talks about the two lives we each have – our inner life, which comes alive *'when you're walking alone or sitting quietly or listening to a piece of music'*, and our outer life, when *'you're going, hello world, here I am, I'm doing lots of things, watch me do them'*. And she has found that it's better to *'let the inner life lead, and let the outer life conform to it'*.

She's specifically talking about what she calls the *'hunches within us'*, deep-seated urges that can guide us to what we will find most gratifying. *'People look for good jobs with good hours and pensions, and none of that is going to be relevant to how you feel about your life. It really isn't.'* She counsels that life is more nourishing if we follow our instincts instead.

But we have to listen carefully for this quieter, inner guide. To this end, she advocates deliberately making the time and space to let such voices be heard. She tells me that she has recently come back from a month by herself in a tiny one-bedroom cottage, to just write and spend time with herself. *'While I was there my social life consisted of walking to the stream at the bottom of the garden. Most of us are normally choked with activities, so bouts of solitariness can be very rewarding.'* Building in such time to just be means that *'really extraordinary things can crop up in your head that you didn't know were there, sort of like waking dreams, fantasies, ambitions. They come out of somewhere that is pre-language, and finding your way back to that place is very important. Once you start articulating ideas in words you've already lost some of the options.'*

It's surprising to hear someone who is professionally eloquent recommending getting back to a pre-language, wordless state, but she says it is a characteristic of anyone creative she's ever known. And she believes we all benefit from allowing time for things to settle, ferment and rise to the top. *'The answer to most people's problems tend to be embedded somewhere inside themselves already and will make themselves felt if given the opportunity to.'*

The one counter point she makes to the importance of our inner guide is that you have to keep an element of critique as well. There should be no self-delusion; you need to be clear-sighted about what you can and cannot do. And there also has to be, at some point, action. She is not advocating spending the rest of your life daydreaming by the stream at the bottom of the garden.

The advice she passes on reflects this view on life and is the same advice she has always given her children:

> **'If you put your head on a pillow late at night and think it hasn't been a good day, wake up next day and change something. It might be your ideas or attitude, it might be to leave a job or husband. It could be anything, but change something. Don't just drag on a set of circumstances which just aren't falling into the right places. You've got to listen to and then act on that inner spark.'**

It's an approach that taps into her first point about ageing: if you nourish your inner self and act in line with it, *'you can go on being as fruitful and as full of ideas as the day is long. You're only declining if you think you are.'*

She cites Robert Plant, her neighbour, as an unexpected inspiration in this regard. *'He's fantastic, incredibly productive, and he's sensational to look at too, very rugged, like Mick Jagger, and with this incredible hair. He's showing no signs of these so-called declining years at all.'*

And neither, it has to be said, is Joan Bakewell.

'IF YOU PUT YOUR HEAD
ON A PILLOW LATE AT NIGHT
AND THINK IT HASN'T BEEN
A GOOD DAY, WAKE UP
NEXT DAY AND CHANGE
SOMETHING. IT MIGHT BE
YOUR IDEAS OR ATTITUDE,
IT MIGHT BE TO LEAVE A
JOB OR A HUSBAND.

IT COULD BE ANYTHING, BUT
CHANGE SOMETHING. DON'T
JUST DRAG ON A SET OF
CIRCUMSTANCES WHICH JUST
AREN'T FALLING INTO THE
RIGHT PLACES. YOU'VE GOT
TO LISTEN TO AND THEN ACT
ON THAT INNER SPARK.'

– *Joan Bakewell*

AHMED 'KATHY' KATHRADA AND DENIS GOLDBERG, FREEDOM FIGHTERS

I ENTER THE MAYFAIR HOTEL ROOM to interview Ahmed 'Kathy' Kathrada and Denis Goldberg, two of Nelson Mandela's fellow freedom fighters, who stood trial and were imprisoned with him for nearly three decades of hard labour. The first thing that is pointed out to me is the modestly sized bed.

'That bed is bigger than the cells we were kept in on Robben Island for twenty-seven years.'

In a small, simple way it brings to mind some of the deprivations these men endured in dedicating their lives to fighting apartheid in South Africa.

Between them they have experienced the worst of what humans do to one another – torture, violence, the murdering of loved ones, unjust imprisonment, solitary confinement, thirty years of separation from their families (Denis's wife was allowed to visit twice in the whole period of his imprisonment).

Despite these experiences, not once did they withdraw from the fight. They made a pledge as young men to overthrow apartheid and they spent every waking hour of the next sixty years doing so.

So where did this commitment to cause, this resilience to hardship come from?

Kathy can pinpoint the moment. It was aged twenty-two, on a visit to Auschwitz as a young man after the end of the Second World War. Here, among the profoundly disturbing reality of what had happened (evidenced by the human bones still scattered casually around the ground), that a dark truth dawned upon him. *'Stood there, I realised that the logical conclusion of racism was genocide. It became clear to me we had to end apartheid to prevent the same happening to the South African people.'* After seeing what he saw, and having reached the conclusion he did, it meant he had to take up and never give up the fight.

An understanding of the history of man's struggle for freedom also helped to form their resolve. Denis recounts that as a young white man he was raised by socially aware parents who not only made sure he respected all people who came to their house irrespective of colour, but also educated him about the Gandhi-led movement for Indian independence, told tales of the lesser-known German resistance and explained the hundred years of struggle by indigenous South Africans against British colonisation. These stories of resistance against an oppressor inspired him and showed him that freedom was not only worth fighting for, it could also ultimately be won.

They are two of the most remarkable men imaginable. As they recount without any bitterness the extreme costs of their sixty-year fight, the humour remains constant (How did you manage to cope with the hardship of prison? '*We got lots of practice.*') and their energy and fight is undimmed.

The morning before we met, Denis had been invited to 10 Downing Street to meet David Cameron. Denis's opening salvo to the Prime Minister: '*So when are you bloody Imperial Brits going to stop beating up on South Africa?*'

Denis is the more fiery of the two gentlemen. In some ways his story is even more pronounced, as he was a white man fighting for an end to apartheid, which was virtually unheard of and meant he was shunned by his own community in a way the other fighters were not. But all men paid the same price for fighting for freedom: life imprisonment.

In fact, even worse had been expected. During the infamous Rivonia court case (1963–64), where Denis, Kathy, Nelson Mandela, Andrew Mlangeni and others stood trial for their action against the South African apartheid regime, everyone expected them to receive the death penalty. They had signed up to their campaign from the beginning knowing it was the most likely outcome.

Following a three-hour speech by Nelson Mandela, the final verdict shocked everyone: life imprisonment. When Denis's mother, who was hard of hearing, called from the gallery, 'What is it? What's the verdict?' Denis replied, 'It's life. Life is wonderful!', a response which gives a sense of the undying resilience and granite-hewn optimism of the men.

An uncomfortable lump in my throat forms as I consider that this moment of relief was then followed by more than twenty years in prison, experiencing the hardest of incarcerations.

Understandably, they prefer to dwell on the outcome, not the experience, the victory, not the battle.

So I ask them about how they achieved the success. What brought about the end of apartheid? With totally clarity, the men cite four factors: the armed struggle, which meant the government undermined itself by increasingly spending more and more money on fighting its own people; themselves as political prisoners, which gave the movement respected figureheads unjustly treated; the international solidarity movement, where governments and civil organisations boycotted South Africa and signalled their opposition to the regime; and finally, the people's struggle in South Africa – the United Democratic Front, the trade unions, civic organisations – the majority of the country coming together to protest, to disrupt, to say No More.

Kathy is clear that, of the four aspects, the mass struggle was the most important. As Nelson Mandela said to the Minister of Justice from his prison cell in Robben Island, 'The future of South Africa can be by bloodshed and in the end the majority will win, or it can be by a negotiated settlement.' With the majority of the people actively protesting and pushing for change, the government eventually conceded.

When I ask what has been the main lesson from their most remarkable of lives, the answers are the most profound of all I have heard.

From Denis:

'I am going to quote John Stuart Mills from the mouth of Nelson Mandela, "To be free it is not sufficient to cast

off your chains, you must so live that you respect and enhance the freedom of others." It's the same concept of what Archbishop Desmond Tutu calls Ubuntu. I am who I am only through others in society. We're humans in the end, and that's what it's all about.'

And then Kathy quietly, gently but definitively states his truth:

'And ultimately, the fight for justice will inevitably lead to success. No matter what the sacrifices are.'

As these men know.

LILY EBERT,
AUSCHWITZ SURVIVOR

'*W*E WEREN'T SEEN AS ENEMIES, *we weren't seen as humans, to the Nazis we were just cockroaches. They completely industrialised their killing of us.*'

I'm sitting talking with Lily Ebert in a quiet room in North London's Holocaust Survivors Centre, the first of its kind in the world. Lily is a proud, defiant, eloquent lady, but as she recounts her experience of Auschwitz she pauses many times. Seventy years on, the pain of mankind's most horrific genocide remains acute. As Lily says, '*It is very difficult to explain something that is unexplainable.*'

'*The lucky ones died*' is her reflection on the transportation to Auschwitz: hundreds of people rammed into railway cattle trucks in the heat of the summer, with no food or water for five days, surrounded by the dead bodies of those who didn't make it. Lily recounts the last thing her mother did before the train arrived. She made Lily swap shoes with her. Hidden within the heel was a small piece of gold, the last of their family's possessions. Call it a mother's intuition, but when they arrived at Auschwitz, Dr Mengele, the Angel of Death, separated the masses into two groups: half were sent left to what would be their immediate death in the gas chambers, and the others were sent right to the slow death of starvation in the camp. Lily's last memory of her mother, younger brother and sister is of seeing them being pushed left.

Inside the camp, Lily and her two younger sisters were stripped of their clothes and dressed in rags, fed on one piece of bread a day and housed in sheds crammed with ten times the number of people they were built for. Every day there were constant 'selections', where anyone deemed not fit enough to work was sent off to the crematorium next door.

Lily says the worst thing of all was the terrible smell emitted from that factory-like building, with the chimney that smoked twenty-four hours a day. It was only when she asked some fellow campmates what was made there that people explained that it wasn't a factory, it was where they burnt Jews, and the only way out of Auschwitz was up that chimney. *'We told them they were mad, that we didn't believe them. But very quickly we found out it was true.'*

In the hell of this experience, Lily promised herself that if she did somehow manage to survive she would spend the rest of her life telling people about Auschwitz so it couldn't happen again. A promise she is keeping for the thousandth time by telling me her story today. That sense of purpose and the responsibility she felt to look after her two younger sisters gave her reason to stay alive in a place where she would otherwise rather have been dead.

It also gives context to one of the pieces of advice she wants to pass on: *'To always have hope against hope. I was as down as a human being can go but look at me, I survived. I have gone from nearly starving to death to, seventy years later, being sent to meet the Queen and being given a BEM. So no matter how bad the situation, try to do what you can and don't give up.'*

However, her most precious piece of advice is:

'Make always the best from what you have, no matter how little it is.'

She brings the thought alive by referring back to that one piece of bread they each had to survive on each day. *'Some in the camp could not make the best of it, they ate it in a second and they dreamed to have something else, but there was nothing else, and they were the ones that didn't survive. I would always eat the one piece of bread as slowly as possible and keep some for the morning hidden under my arm. And that helped me survive.'*

At the end of our meeting, Lily proudly shows me a small gold pendant round her neck, which she has worn every day since being freed. She explains it is the piece of gold that her mother hid in her shoe, which she managed to keep hidden throughout her whole time in Auschwitz.

I reflect on what this piece of gold and its owner have seen and had to endure. The starvation, the brutal conditions, the worst of mankind. But it also creates a small question in my mind: given that she lost her shoes in the camp, how did she manage to keep the piece of gold? Eyes sparkling with triumph, Lily says: *'I told you, you have to make the best of whatever you have. The only thing I had was that piece of bread, so I hid the gold every night in that and they never spotted it. I was cleverer than them.'*

Lily Ebert: pure gold.

'MAKE ALWAYS THE BEST
FROM WHAT YOU HAVE,
NO MATTER HOW LITTLE IT
IS . . . I WOULD ALWAYS EAT
THE ONE PIECE OF BREAD
AS SLOWLY AS POSSIBLE AND
KEEP SOME FOR THE MORNING
HIDDEN UNDER MY ARM.
AND THAT HELPED
ME SURVIVE.'

– Lily Ebert

THE HEART-BREAKING GENIUS
OF RICHARD CURTIS

I F THE OSCARS HAD A category for Best Human, Richard Curtis would get nominated. Not for the pleasure his script-writing has brought to the masses, abundant though that is, with *Four Weddings and a Funeral, Notting Hill, Love, Actually* and other such treasures to his name, but for his decades-long commitment as co-founder, leader and/or chief agitator for such era-defining social initiatives as Comic Relief, Red Nose Day, Make Poverty History and Live 8. No other person has done more to make development aid and charity part of the mainstream.

From such an evolved human being, I have high hopes for his best piece of advice, especially when he says he's thought about it in advance and committed his wisdom to paper. *'So here it is,'* he says, as he opens his writerly, leather-bound notebook. He sits forward, clears his throat and announces:

'Don't let your mum cut your hair. That's important.'

Closes book, sits back.

He's serious, sort of. *'My mum did mine once and I didn't talk to her for three weeks.'* This recollection triggers a follow-up insight. *'And if you're a mum, don't cut your son's hair, he'll hate you.'*

It's not just his wisdom on hairdos that is rooted in childhood, most key attributes of his life have an invisible string that, when pulled, brings up a story from his younger years. He confesses to having scripted so many romantic movies *'because I had my heart broken at university'*, and he writes a 'Hapless Bernard' into every movie, an in joke-revenge of a man who once stole his girlfriend.

More significantly, it was during one of his younger, love-struck, feeling-sorry-for-himself moments that his father said something that changed Richard's perspective on life in general. *'My dad, not unkindly, described his own life at eighteen, which was finding himself fatherless and cleaning toilets on a ship to earn money, and compared it to what my life was like. And I was absolutely fixed after that. It gave me a sense of perspective between my problems and other people's that I have kept forever.'*

A second slice of childhood wisdom from his dad has also reverberated through his life: *'He always said you can't be happier than happy.'* The idea that if you are content and things are good, do not be disturbed by the possibility that they could be better. *'Don't let a lovely day out in the countryside be ruined by the fact that it's not sunny.'*

As with his movies, though, there is a twist. *'I say that, but I am an unhappy person almost all the time.'* I assume he's joking, but in response to my protestations he explains that raising money for the development of the world's poorest nations means he gets his heart re-broken several times a day.

'With the charity work I feel the pressure of every phone call, that if I can talk this person into doing something, kids survive, if I don't, they won't. Just today I got a call from a lovely guy saying he won't be able

to do a sketch and of course I have to lie and say "It's OK, you helped last year," but inside I am dying.'

So his best piece of advice comes directly from his experience of trying to change the world, but also reflects the frustration and heartbreak that comes from knowing people talk a good game but often fail to help when the need for aid is so vast.

> *'None of us should ever underestimate our ability to change people's lives. There is a direct cause and effect of what we do here and what happens there. But if you want to help you have to actually do something. You can't just talk about it. My motto is "If you want to make things happen, you have to make things." Create an object, a slogan, a film, a little book, a badge, a hashtag, a Red Nose Day . . . make something so wonderful that it captures people's hearts and minds so they can't help but be dragged in and help. And even better, make it funny too. That's all I have ever done.'*

And there is no one who does it better.

JUDE KELLY FOR EVERYONE

OR SOMEONE RUNNING ONE OF the world's largest and
most complex cultural institutions, Jude Kelly, artistic
director of the UK's Southbank Centre, has a simple
description of what she does. *'I tell stories. That's what I have been
doing all my life.'*

It is a statement she means literally. Throughout her career she
has directed more than a hundred plays, including for the Royal
Shakespeare Company and in the West End, and now has the
biggest job in the arts in the UK, but it all started with her as a
young girl putting on plays in her back garden, using the neigh-
bours' children as cast members and their parents as an audience.

Those childhood plays not only gave clarity on what to do
with her life (at the age of eleven she declared she was going to
be a theatre director and has been making it happen ever since),
but those early exploits also provided the defining attribute of
her approach to story-telling: the absolute imperative of making
the arts fully inclusive. *'I loved the idea that the whole neighbourhood
would gather together to watch the plays, and I felt very upset if everyone
wasn't there. I hate people being left out. Not just for their sake, but for
our sake too.'*

It is an organising principle that has driven Jude ever since: that both the community and the art of that community are better served when everyone is included. *'We need people with different life experiences so we can hear each other's stories, to add to them, to understand them, to disagree with them, to help people stop feeling self-conscious about bumping into other tribes and help people feel there could be something richer if they experiment with other human relationships.'* In short, making the arts inclusive deepens society's empathy and cohesion.

The Southbank Centre is publicly funded, which furthers her resolve to make all welcome: *'The whole of society pays into the pot, so everybody needs to get a slice: that is my absolute driving energy and belief system.'* And she delivers. On the day I visit the Southbank there is a Pram Jam for parents with young children, an Indian performance artist, a classical concert by refugee musicians, a banging techno night, Jeremy Irons reciting Shakespeare, an a capella beat-boxing show, a circus, some stand-up comedy and a street-food market. Something, in other words, for everyone.

Jude also has a parallel role as founder and leader of Women of the World, a global festival that celebrates women and girls and looks at the obstacles they face. It fits with her mission of getting everyone included, with a clear focus, in this case, on gender equality. She says her awareness of the ever-present issue has been heightened by being a female leader and the sheer number of times young women have come to *'ask for advice on the things they were struggling with: work/life balance, whether to have children, what would happen to them if they did, the way they were treated at work, the way they were treated by partners, issues of violence, rape, online porn, body image, it goes on and on, but also positive stories too, things women and girls have achieved'*. So she decided to start the festival as a place for people to come together, talk about their issues, feel positive and explore what gender equality could one day look like.

Amazingly, she originally received some resistance to the idea. *'When I started the festival people said "Really? Haven't we already done gender equality?" But I knew we hadn't done it by any means. And that was before Malala was shot, before Boko Haram had captured the Nigerian girls, before the Delhi gang rapes, so we need to pick up the stone and look under it. But also celebrate the things that have been achieved, the wonderful stories too, so it gives us stamina and energy.'*

Jude says the issue has to be tackled in the arts, too. *'Most plays, most films, most novels, most artworks historically have been by men, and there's always been a central doubt expressed over and over again, can women be truly creative compared to men? Historically there has been a view that says, well, women have children, that's their creativity. It's a version of the same thinking that says black people have strong bodies but they're not very intelligent, or the Chinese are very clever but don't have an emotional life, all these damaging stereotypes framing half the human race inside a patriarchal power structure that has been inherited and internalised over thousands of years.'*

This mission to tackle and defeat the ingrained issue of gender equality is much more than a day job. It strikes me as the story she will most want told about her life, and in keeping with such a script she offers her most valuable piece of advice about, and to, women:

'WOMEN HAVE TO HONOUR
THEIR OWN POTENTIAL.
WOMEN MUST GIVE
THEMSELVES THE RIGHT
TO THRIVE IN EVERY SINGLE
WAY, AND NOT DEFINE HOW
LOVING OR HUMBLE THEY
ARE BY THE AMOUNT THAT
THEY ARE PREPARED TO STEP
SIDEWAYS TO ACCOMMODATE

SOMEONE ELSE. THEY NEED
TO SAY, "I'VE GOT ONE LIFE,
I'VE BEEN GIVEN LIFE, IT HAS
BEEN BREATHED INTO ME
AND HERE I AM AND I
SHOULD USE IT FOR THE
BEST POSSIBLE PURPOSE."
WHATEVER EACH WOMAN
HERSELF DEFINES THAT TO BE.'

– *Jude Kelly*

MICHAEL McINTYRE,
YES MAN

I'M ON THE PHONE TRYING to arrange a meeting with Michael McIntyre, the highest-grossing comedian in the world, but I can't: he's making me laugh too much. The experience, however, is at least answering a question I've always asked myself: are professional comedians funny when they're not on stage? In this case, the answer is: oh yes.

When we finally do meet in person, it continues. Michael starts by noting that I'm talking too loudly for a restaurant – almost as noisily as an *American*, he adds in a faux-bitchy whisper. He confesses to suffering from what he calls *'restaurant hush'*, the British middle class need to speak quietly when you are somewhere a bit posh.

Surprisingly, for a chat with one of the world's funniest men, we quickly get into the topic of financial planning: the importance of never spending more than you earn, of avoiding the perils of credit cards and compounding interest. The reason: as a struggling stand-up he spent ten painful years spiralling into debt before making it big. *'By the time I was thirty my career had gone nowhere and I'd got myself £40,000 in the hole. I was sitting in my room and thought, my life is not my life, I'm renting everything: the flat's rented, the furniture's on credit, the TV I'm paying off at Dixons . . . even that video needs to go back to Blockbusters.'*

It's funny material now but was serious back then. The bailiffs were called in. The first time they took his car, then the furniture, then his appliances. On one visit he realised there was a man with a boom microphone accompanying the debt collector. When Michael queried the recording equipment, he explained he was making a documentary about bailiffs for Radio 4. *'I said, "I can't be in that," but then I thought maybe this could be the break I'm looking for, so I started to try and be funny, thinking maybe if I'm on the radio someone will get in touch.'*

So what took him from those dire straits to centre stage? A simple but fundamental thing happened: he had Lucas, his first child. According to Michael, comedians get funnier when they become parents, mainly because they have to. For him the effect was instant: the sense of responsibility, the need to provide. *'I thought I'm going to do whatever it takes to make it before he can speak. I don't want his first words to be, "Daddy, why is that man taking the video recorder?"'*

So the motivation was clear, but how does a comedian actually make themselves funnier?

'I was crazed with it. I started doing gigs seven nights a week, for less money, for no money, just to keep practising, to get the jokes together, and to get the stage time. I knew if I could get one big laugh, then if I worked hard enough I'd get another and then another.'

Over time he built a twenty-minute set he considered bullet-proof (*'I could make twelve people in a room above a pub who weren't really listening start to cry with laughter'*), then he rang up the biggest agent in comedy, got him down to a gig in a small club, and gave the best and most important performance of his life.

When he came off the stage, the agent simply said, *'You're a revelation,'* and booked him for his first TV gig on the Royal Variety Performance. And then, boom. Like most overnight successes, it had taken ten years for him to get there.

Getting the stage time, never mind screen time, is somewhat easier now for Michael, as the country's most in-demand comedian. But he still works the small gig circuit, doing dingy clubs on rainy Tuesday nights whenever he's crafting new material. And he still remembers how painful it can be when you don't have the money, when things aren't working, when the situation is looking pretty hopeless. So he passes on this advice to those at that stage:

'You somehow need to find a way to believe, to keep going. But it's not enough to just say to yourself "be confident", you can't just BE confident, you have to surround yourself with people who bring the best from you, who will help you, who will help you grow that confidence. I'm like **Britain's Got Talent.** *I need my three yeses. I need my wife, my mother and my agent to all say, "Yes, that was good." Then it's like, all right, that works, I can keep going. I put my success down to that: my wife, my family, my support network. My three yeses.'*

This time, he's not joking.

NOELLA COURSARIS MUSUNKA, MODEL CITIZEN

THE DEMOCRATIC REPUBLIC OF THE Congo is a contradiction rendered as a country. It has more natural resources than any other nation in the world, but is one of the poorest in GDP and life expectancy. It has enough latent hydro-power to fuel most of Africa, but less than 10 per cent of homes have electricity. It has an image in the West of a barren, war-stricken land of heinous crimes, but is one of the most verdant and beautiful countries you could ever hope to visit, with people as friendly and welcoming as any on earth, a fact I can attest to, not just from having spent time there but also because I am sitting opposite one of the DRC's favourite daughters.

The lady in question is Noella Coursaris Musunka, the international model who splits her time between fashion shoots for *Vogue* and Agent Provocateur and a parallel life running Malaika, an organisation she founded, providing education and schooling to young girls in the DRC.

Noella's backstory is that of a woman who has known tough times. She was born to a desperately poor family in the Congo and lost her father at the age of five. In a country where seven million kids don't go to school and where life expectancy is just forty-eight, her mother took the understandable decision to send her to be raised by her aunt in Europe. But Noella never forgot her childhood and her home, and has used the currency of her modelling career to become one of the brightest lights and biggest advocates for her country of birth.

She was motivated to combine her career in fashion with tackling education in the DRC for defiantly positive reasons. *'I'm a spokesperson for the beliefs that I want for my country. I want children to be taught that they are living in an amazing country, an amazing continent – that we have nothing to envy in any way.'* At the sharper end, she also wants the people of the Congo to benefit more from the resources of their country. *'If you get on a plane in the Congo, it's full of Americans, English, Chinese and Indians, but very few Africans, it's mad. It seems a lot of people love our resources!'* she says laughing, but meaning it.

Ultimately Noella wants to help end the era where Africa is treated as 'less than' the rest of the world and, to do so, education is the answer. *'Through quality education our own people can become agents of change, become leaders of their own country, so we can work with the West as equals, that is what's missing.'*

She makes no boast about the scale of her work. At the end of the day, she is educating just thousands of children in a country that is failing millions, but it is a start. And she uses her voice and the platform of her career to agitate others to do the same. This mission of encouraging others to act, to get involved, to do something rather than nothing, is inherent in her advice.

'Any voice you have in this world, you have to use it. Whatever money you have the day you die, you die without it, so donate it. If you can only give an hour of your time, then do that.'

— *Noella Coursaris Musunka*

UP ALL NIGHT
WITH INDRA NOOYI

WHAT DO YOU DO WHEN 'the Most Powerful Woman in the World', as ranked by *Forbes Magazine*, invites you to dinner? You say yes, of course. The woman in question was Indra Nooyi, the Global CEO of PepsiCo and board member of the Federal Reserve. The context was that Innocent, the juice business started by myself and two friends, had been growing fast and, unknown to us, had got us on the radar of some of the major food and drinks companies. Indra's people called us out of the blue and said she would like to meet. They suggested dinner next time she was in London.

It seemed churlish to say no, and I was curious about what it took to be a global CEO of a business responsible for operations across the planet, with hundreds of thousands of employees, creating opportunities and issues in every time zone. How did she manage the workload? What was life like? Did she have any good advice? The dinner proved illuminating on all three fronts.

We started the evening with polite chit-chat, questions like 'So how long are you in London for?' and other such conversational placeholders. Interestingly, it turned out Indra was leaving that evening, as soon as we finished dinner. Her private jet was fired up and ready to go and would be heading from London to New York after our coffees and mints. Meanwhile, her husband, another global CEO of a big tech company, had *his* private jet in New York also ready to go, destination London. They had two daughters and a rule that one parent should always be at home with them, and were timing flights so that when she took off, he would too. At around 1 a.m. that night, somewhere above the Atlantic, they would pass each other at a combined velocity of a thousand miles per hour, like proverbial (extremely fast) ships in the night. I found the image memorable. As I did the idea of a two-jet household.

When we got on to her approach to work, she spoke with total passion. She deeply loved what she did, and she did it a lot. At one point in the conversation, Indra asked, *'You know that buzz you get when you haven't been to sleep for three nights because you've been working on a deal?'* I had to admit to her I did not. In fact, I said, I didn't even know what the buzz from staying up for just one night was like – well, not for work anyway – an answer that momentarily perplexed her.

She told me that she'd once done eight nights straight without going to bed, such was the size of the deal she was working on. I queried whether this was even physiologically possible, and she admitted, under my cross-examination, she had grabbed fifteen minutes on her office couch on the eighth night. To this day, I still don't know if she was playing mind games on me. If she was, it worked. I thought that if that's what it takes to be a global CEO, I'd better stay a local one.

She was brilliant company: charming, eloquent, engaging, but capable of saying the most unexpected things. When I got to asking her advice, she first wanted to dispense a few leadership tips, the most memorable of which was: *'I get my board to come round to my house once a month and I print out song sheets and we all sing songs together. I really recommend you do the same.'* When I said I wanted her single most valuable piece of advice, this is what she offered.

> **'Don't take holidays. When you get to my age you will regret taking them. Give yourself a maximum of a day or a day and a half a year. And use that to read books on your industry. The rest of the time you should just work.'**

The first thing I thought was, 'Wow, that's genuinely the worst piece of advice I've ever heard.' The second thing I thought was, 'You need to go on holiday more often.' I was going to say just that, but then with my third thought I remembered that she was 'the Most Powerful Woman in the World', so I just kept quiet, nodded and ate my pudding.

INDRA NOOYI

❖

233

'DON'T TAKE HOLIDAYS. WHEN
YOU GET TO MY AGE YOU WILL
REGRET TAKING THEM. GIVE
YOURSELF A MAXIMUM OF A
DAY OR A DAY AND

A HALF A YEAR. AND USE THAT
TO READ BOOKS ON YOUR
INDUSTRY. THE REST OF THE
TIME YOU SHOULD JUST WORK.'

— *Indra Nooyi*

FACE TIME WITH UELI STECK

THE NORTH FACE OF THE Eiger is the most infamous climb in the world. It's known in the mountaineering community as 'The Wall of Death', a mile-high, concave cliff-face covered with ice, loose rocks and tragedy: as difficult and as unforgiving to climb as it sounds and looks.

The first two people ever to attempt climbing it died trying. And so did the next four, starting a death tally that currently stands at sixty-five. When a group did eventually summit the North Face, it took them more than three *days*. I give this historical context because Ueli Steck, the Swiss climber I'm currently with, recently did it in under three *hours*, an unimaginable speed made possible only by his gravity- (and sanity-) defying decision to do it *without* ropes. It was an achievement so disproportionate, so unprecedented in the annals of mountaineering, that it didn't just rewrite the rules of climbing, it seemed also to rewrite the laws of physics.

As an amateur climber myself (and I strongly emphasise the word 'amateur') I tell him I struggle with his decision to climb without ropes, which are the only hope you have of remaining safe if you make a mistake and fall (which, in my experience, happens often).

'I remember when I started climbing and I heard there were people climbing without ropes I thought to myself that's insane, I will never do that. But it's a process, figuring out stuff, doing it better, and that's what drives me.'

But what about the chance element you can't control? *'You just have to accept it, you have to commit.'* And the fear? *'When I'm climbing, there is no fear. If you feel fear, it's because you're not well prepared.'*

As advice goes, it sounds potentially like bravado, but in Ueli's case it's not. In fact, in Ueli's view having bravado is deadly: you need an absence of ego to stay safe. *'You have to make sure you feel no pressure to get to the top otherwise you start making the wrong decisions. On a climbing day, I always say "I'll just go and have a look." I never say, "I am going to do it." And if I have a bad feeling, I just come back down. I believe if you stick to that then you never make a mistake.'*

Of course, with Ueli's approach to climbing there literally can never be a mistake, not one.

> **'I really play on the edge. The time on the Eiger, I had to move fast, so I allow myself to hit only once with the ice axe, no compromise, never twice. Full commitment each time I place the axe. And it works, you really concentrate, you really hit precise.'**

It's a way of thinking that turns inside out what other human beings would do: if you were a mile up a vertical cliff-face and your life depended on the ice axe you're about to put all your weight on, you'd want to check it would hold. Ueli instead uses the consequences of what it would mean if it won't, to make sure he concentrates hard enough to place it correctly in the first place. That is some advanced-level psychology.

On a deeper level, that degree of commitment is perhaps partly enabled by his personal take on the potential consequence. *'If I fuck up, it's over. I'm dead and I don't have to live with my mistake.'* Amazingly, he says he would rather have that outcome than, say, the pressure of being a CEO, *'where if you screw up, you have to fire people and they lose their jobs and you know it was your fault and you have to live with that your whole lifetime. I don't know if I could handle that.'*

It's a final comment that reinforces the huge gap between myself and Ueli. I have actually climbed the Eiger – it took me two days and was by the incomparably easier Western ridge, and involved a lot of ropes and guides, and there were still plenty of moments when, clinging trembling to the rock, I would have happily fired my own grandmother to get off that damn mountain.

But I decide not to mention that to Ueli.

MARGARET ATWOOD, AGONY AUNT

OOKING BACK, I HAD AN itch of apprehension before
making the call. I was due to interview Margaret Atwood,
the Canadian-born, internationally renowned Booker
Prize-winning novelist; a soothsayer and chronicler with the
wisdom that comes from being over forty books old. To gen up,
I read a couple of interviews online, but they throw up two
uncomfortably pertinent facts: firstly, she hates choosing favourites
of any kind, and secondly she doesn't believe in giving advice.
The reason for my call? To ask for her favourite piece of advice.

The phone call starts well enough. We talk of Pelee Island, a
tiny gathering of land in Lake Erie, south-west of Toronto. She's
recently been hosting the annual 'Spring Song' there, a bird race
and book-reading event that raises money for the Pelee Island
Heritage Centre while drawing attention to the migratory birds
that use the island to rest their weary wings. Margaret empathises
with them: the island offers her respite too, and a place to write
with few distractions: *'The locals point tourists looking for our house
ten kilometres in the wrong direction.'*

But I know I can't hide behind this island talk for long, so I outline my plans for the book, explaining that I am looking for her best piece of advice. Like all her answers, it comes quick and complete. *'Oh, I never give advice unless I'm asked for it.'* But it's a better response than I am expecting, so I point out that I *am* asking.

Unfortunately, it is not the key to the conversation I was hoping it might be. *'OK, but what are you asking advice about? Advice needs to be specific. For all I know, you could be looking for advice on how to open a jar.'* I explain that I'm OK with overly protective lids (run under a hot tap or gently hit the side to loosen), I'm more looking for advice that she particularly holds to be true or useful in life generally. *'Yes, but for who? For what? Advice always relates to the person and the situation. For a start, what if you suffer from depression? That can make a massive difference to how you are in life and what you might need or find helpful.'* Ah, I wasn't expecting *that.* I know 25 per cent of people suffer from mental illness and I don't want to imply a sentence or two of wisdom will somehow solve their issues. So I tell her I take her point, and say let's assume we're talking about the other 75 per cent. *'OK. So are these people born to loving parents or not? That is another huge impact on our lives and I think my advice would differ depending on that factor.'* Hmm, now where? On the one hand I agree that a few words of advice are a poor substitute for not being loved as a child, but on the other hand, it's going to bugger things up for me and my book if I can't get a piece of advice out of Margaret Atwood.

I take some solace from her tone. She is not coming across as someone whose aim is to undermine, she actually seems engaged and keen to help. In fact, it appears she'll happily do *anything* for me, with the exception of one thing. It's just unfortunate that it happens to be the only thing I want of her.

I decide to call on God for help. *'Look,'* I begin, *'if you take religion, you can essentially boil its better teachings down into some human behaviours that are universally beneficial to all.'*

'Ah yes, love thy neighbour, forgive one another, that kind of thing?'

'Yes, exactly,' I enthusiastically reply, thinking *now* we're getting somewhere. My optimism proves short-lived.

'Trouble is, I'm more of a revenge kind of gal myself. But when someone smites me I'm normally too lazy to do anything about it. I tend to let karma take care of things.'

OK, so religion didn't work. I try psychology. I give a simplistic overview of studies into human happiness, which show that people who help others end up feeling happier about themselves. Isn't there something in that?

'Sure, unless you do it too much, and then you end up exhausting yourself, and that doesn't help anyone.'

I'm now starting to confront the uncomfortable truth that I am dealing with someone on the other end of the phone who is just plain smarter and of quicker wit than me. I'm basically in a verbal fencing match with one of the greatest writers alive, and, as you would expect, I am losing.

Margaret senses I'm on the ropes and decides to give me a breather. *'Look,'* she explains, *'I'm a novelist. In my world, everything is about the character. Who are they, where are they? Are they old or young, rich or poor? What do they want? Until I know what they are wrestling with, how can I give advice?'*

'President Clinton managed to,' I protest.

Margaret's interested. *'Oh, and what did he say?'* I recount his advice of the importance of seeing everyone: the person who pours your coffee, the person who opens the door for you. I say it's a piece of advice that strikes me as something relevant to all humans. *'Unless they're a writer trying to get a book finished, then I'd tell them the last thing you need is to see people more, you need to stay home and work.'*

The conversation has the feel of a cat playing with a mouse. And I'm not the one purring. I resort to pleading: given all that you've learnt, there must be something you think is worth passing on.

'OK, I've got something for you. How about this: "When it comes to cactii, it's the small spikes that get you, not the big ones.'

'Is that a metaphor for life?' I ask hopefully.

'No, no, I mean it literally, I was just in the garden doing the weeding before you called and those little devils are painful.' I explain that it may be a little too specific for this book, but I'll bear it in mind for a future volume on gardening tips.

I'm conscious I'm nearly out of time. I have one last go. Still wanting to help, Margaret asks me one more time to focus down the audience for this intended advice. I confess I haven't narrowed my intended audience down any further than to my fellow *Homo sapiens*. Margaret lets out a short, sharp laugh. *'But aren't you then just talking about a book of trite sayings that you'd read in the toilet, full of things like, "Make a smiley face and you'll feel more smiley"?'*

'Of course not,' I reply.

But secretly I think to myself, maybe I can just use that.

'I'M A NOVELIST. IN MY WORLD, EVERYTHING IS ABOUT THE CHARACTER. WHO ARE THEY, WHERE ARE THEY? ARE THEY OLD OR YOUNG, RICH OR POOR? WHAT DO THEY WANT? UNTIL I KNOW WHAT THEY ARE WRESTLING WITH, HOW CAN I GIVE ADVICE?'

– Margaret Atwood

THE NEW TONY BLAIR

THERE'S BEEN A SMALL CHANGE in wardrobe since I last met Tony Blair. Back then, he was in Office, and sporting classic PM-wear: smart suit, crisp shirt, party-loyal tie. Now, in his post-premiership world, things have loosened up a little: sports jacket, blue jeans, open-necked shirt. There's also a pretty healthy suntan going on. Life after Office seems to be treating him well. Tony Blair is looking *good*.

The same can be said of his private offices too, tucked into a discreet corner of Grosvenor Square. They are beautifully and stylishly appointed, nicer in fact than the rooms in 10 Downing Street; a benefit that comes from being able to choose your building, rather than the building choosing you.

But while things around him may have changed, Tony Blair has not. His most distinctive quality remains undimmed: a catalysing energy that radiates from him. His enthusiasm, engagement and intellect imbues the room with an intangible sense of more-to-come, that things will only get better. Just being in Tony Blair's presence encourages you to think bigger, to work harder, to do more.

In fact, according to Tony Blair, he's actually working as hard as he ever has, wrestling with some of the world's toughest sudokus – religious extremism, African development, peace in the Middle East. Whatever your views on Tony Blair, the man is committed. There's not a lot of golf going on.

We talk of his time in Office. I say that it seems to me the quintessential experience of being a prime minister is on any given day you work under the most intense and unyielding pressure, and just when you think it can't get any worse, a completely new issue broadsides you, one that you somehow also have to now deal with. And alongside all of this, your rivals in the House and the media are deliberately giving the very worst possible interpretation to your very best intentions. *'Tell me about it,'* he says ruefully. *'I could write a book on that one.'*

Alongside this constant stress and pressure, he says that, as Prime Minister, you also feel *'a sense of inner awe at the magnitude of the decisions you're taking on a daily, even hourly, basis, which you're aware affect the lives of people very deeply'*.

So how does one cope with the relentlessness of it all? Tony lays out his four-point PM plan to keep on an even keel. Firstly, count your blessings. No matter the pressures, don't forget it is an enormous privilege to be doing such a job. Secondly, remember, as his wife Cherie would repeatedly point out, it is voluntary, no one is *forcing* you to be Prime Minister. Thirdly, have a belief in what you are doing, and the people you are doing it for. And fourthly, don't get too up yourself, you need to keep a sense of humour. Keep those four things at the front of your mind and the stress becomes more bearable.

He also advocates making space for what he calls *'some personal hinterland'*: spend time with the family; play the guitar, as he famously did; take holidays. Not that you're ever fully off-duty as Prime Minister. Even on the family vacations, Tony Blair would travel with a small office and every day fulfil some PM responsibilities. In his ten years he never got a whole day off. He'd always be working, even if working on the suntan.

It begs the question: did he actually enjoy being PM? *'Enjoy always struck me as a weird word to use about the job. I would say that I felt a great sense of purpose and passion about it. But enjoy in the sense of pure pleasure? Only at very rare moments, such as securing the Good Friday agreement and winning the Olympics. They felt good. But the main satisfaction came from moving forward on what we wanted to achieve in government, on the programme of reform we set out.'*

This commitment to public service, to helping people, to improving things is clearly the internal engine that powered him through a decade in power. But he hadn't always wanted to be a politician. In fact, it was only when his father-in-law took him into the House of Commons that he discovered this calling, his vocation. *'Stood there in the House, I just got this sense of "This is where I need to be, this is what I need to be doing." I was a lawyer at that time and quite a successful one, but it never gave me that feeling. But once I decided to become an MP, I started waking up with a great sense of purpose every day and it never left me.'*

Which takes us to his very best piece of advice:

'People tend not to be accidentally successful. If you see anyone very, very good at something, they tend to be very

driven by what they do and they work really hard at it.
So find the thing that makes you passionate and do that.
And if you can find something you're passionate about
that also makes a difference to others, it will be a greatly
fulfilling quality in your life. In the end, the things that
give the most fulfilment are the things you do for others.'

'FIND THE THING THAT
MAKES YOU PASSIONATE AND
DO THAT . . . IN THE END, THE
THINGS THAT GIVE THE MOST
FULFILMENT ARE THE THINGS
YOU DO FOR OTHERS.'

— *Tony Blair*

LA *FAMILIA* OF RUTHIE ROGERS

I AM IN THE PLACE WHERE the ley lines of architecture and gastronomy meet: the kitchen of River Cafe co-founder and million-plus cook-book writer Ruthie Rogers, inside her majestic Chelsea home designed by architect husband Richard Rogers.

The open kitchen is the prominent feature of the temple-dimensioned main room, a gleaming stainless steel altar dispensing bread and wine and whatever's in season to hungry, grateful mouths. After a few 'grrr's and hisses from behind the scenes, two expertly made, bitterly dark espressos appear, along with Ruthie herself, the warmth of each matching the other. If you want to find the spirit of hospitality manifested in a person, Ruthie is it.

The River Cafe is an ode to the Italian way of life, where food and *la familia* intertwine. Although Ruthie was born in America, her husband is from Florence and thirty years of holidays in the family's home have infused Ruthie with the passion of Italian cooking. *'I would walk into Richard's aunt's kitchen and find two sisters arguing over whether pappa pomodoro should have water in it or just the tomatoes, and I thought this is the kind of argument I like.'*

Richard's mother, Dada, was dedicated to sharing her secrets of how to cook, eat and live with Ruthie. *'Even on her death bed she was still passing on tips. Her last words to me were "Ruthie, I want you to put more cream on your face and less herbs on your fish."'*

Inspired by this convergence of love, food and family, Ruthie and Rose started the River Cafe as *'a restaurant where we could create the kind of food that we ate in people's homes in Italy'*.

While the River Cafe is now in its third decade and seats hundreds of people a day, it started in the smallest way possible. *'The original space was tiny, only enough to do thirty or forty covers a day. Plus, the council only gave us a licence for lunchtimes Monday to Friday, no evenings, no weekends, and exclusively for the employees in the offices where the restaurant was sited. So we had to sneak customers in, pretending they worked there.'*

However, their ambition was about quality, not size: the goal was to become the best Italian restaurant in London. And word spread quickly about the authenticity of the cooking, even though customers weren't technically allowed to go. Paradoxically, the opening line of the River Cafe's first-ever review (in the *Evening Standard* by Fay Maschler) was, *'I'm going to tell you about a restaurant that you can't go to.'* But, as Ruthie puts it, the restaurant grew as they grew with experience. Over time more space was acquired, planning permissions were gradually improved and it evolved into the big, beautiful restaurant it is today. And that experience is why she advises that if you are going to open a restaurant or business *'start small, think big, grow with control'*.

Part of the enduring success of the restaurant is seeing the team as important an ingredient as any of the seasonally sourced ones coming into the kitchen. *'People often talk to me about how much they love the food, but they always start by saying how good the people were.'* Her advice here is:

> **'Give and you get back what you give. Treat everyone as individuals: understand how people are and encourage them. There is real discipline too underpinning the work they do. I strongly believe that you achieve more in a work environment with hope rather than fear . . . the whole concept of people shouting or bullying or intimidating is foreign to me.'**

This River Cafe family is unusual not just for its closeness but also because, in an industry dominated by men, it was headed by two matriarchs, the second being Ruthie's partner and fellow chef Rose Gray. *'Our relationship was remarkable. We cooked together, worked together, wrote together, went to Italy together, we even wore the same clothes.'* The symbiotic nature of their partnership made Rose's death in 2010 all the more painful, and daunting to deal with. *'Rose was a force. When she died it was like becoming a single parent, but with eighty-five children. But I thought the greatest tribute would be to make the reataurant better and better.'*

One year later Ruthie lost her twenty-six-year-old son, who died suddenly of a seizure in Italy. Ruthie likens this to *'a tsunami. One minute you are safe on the beach looking out to sea, and then it* strikes and you are drowning.' I ask, if there is any advice she can pass on to someone being hit by such a tsunami of their own. Her answer reflects just how terrible an experience it is.

'As much as I would like to, I don't think I can, because people were giving me advice and none of it worked. The only thing that got me through it was the love for my children, the closeness and tightness of our family. I would be somewhere and one of my children would appear. I'd come down in the morning and a friend would be on the sofa. They would just somehow happen to be there for Richard and me.' A beautiful tribute to the power and strength of her close friends and family.

Ruthie sticks with the water analogy and says that five years on 'the waters are still rough, but you learn how to navigate, you learn what you can do, what you can't do, the times you need to be prepared for'. And while it would be misunderstanding the depth of the emotions to say her work provided consolation, it did sometimes help bring distraction. 'I found it too difficult to cook, it was too contemplative, I would stand there stirring the risotto and cry. The nights were better as they were busier.'

And the love and sense of family she had always shown to her team, the insistence she and Rose always had of treating people kindly, respecting them, encouraging them, meant at least she was in an environment that felt safe. 'Obviously nothing is more important than your family, your children, the people you love, but I think that there's an intertwining of work and family with the River Cafe and when I walk in I just think how great they are.'

She pauses for a moment, reflecting on what role the River

Cafe has played in her life. *'People say to me, "Gosh, you're still here," and I think to myself, "Well, where else would I want to be?"'*

Which, to me, sounds like the ultimate measure of success.

'Put more cream
and less herbs

on your face
on your fish.'

— DADA ROGERS,
VIA RUTHIE ROGERS

JONY IVE JUST SAYS NO

UTSIDE SPORT, IT'S HARD TO claim that someone is
genuinely number one in their respective field. How
can you judge who is the best artist, writer, actor or
whatever in the world? Jony Ive, the head of design at Apple Inc.
and the most successful industrial designer of the modern age, is
an exception to this dilemma. He is the man who crafted that
convergence of artistry and technology currently residing in your
pocket, and who worked with the world's most famous and
revered founder to create literally the most valuable company in
existence.

For a man who genuinely is the 'Big I Am', he does not act
like it. I meet him at a burger van eating some chips. Admittedly,
it's a burger van at a private party, and they are very nice chips,
but with his extraordinary success also comes a high degree of
humility and self-deprecation. It seems to be a trait among genuinely successful and credible people: they tend to be, for want of
a better description, nice. He even offered me some of his chips.

I decline on the food, but ask for his number-one piece of
advice instead. It was neither original nor complicated, but it is
probably the single-most important driver of success – and

certainly fits with the laser-like focus of his company:

'You have to really focus. Just do one thing. And aim to become best in the world at it.'

He admits that wasn't necessarily how he used to think. With a brain as creative as Jony's, there are a thousand different things he would want to do. *'I learnt the importance of focus from Steve [Jobs]. His view was you have to say "No" a lot more often than you say "Yes". In fact, he used to ask me each day what I had said "No" to, to check I was stopping things and saying "No" to things and not getting distracted.'*

My favourite thing about this story is that when Jony told it to me he paused and then confessed that he used to make up projects that he could then tell Steve he had stopped, so he always had an example of something he had said 'No' to when Steve came by. Which brings me on to a second thing about successful people, even the brilliant ones: like the rest of us, they are, at times, still faking it a little.

'JUST DO ONE THING.
AND AIM TO BECOME BEST
IN THE WORLD AT IT.'

– Jony Ive

PARENTAL GUIDANCE WITH
BARONESS HELENA KENNEDY QC

'*W*hat *people always say to me, even my mother, is "Why can't you have some nice clients?"'* recounts Helena Kennedy QC, one of the UK's most active and outspoken advocates of civil liberties and human rights. Admittedly, one can understand where that question comes from: her client list is chilli-peppered with the most controversial people in modern British history: the child murderer Myra Hindley, the IRA bombers behind the Brighton Hotel attack that aimed to kill Margaret Thatcher, and the 'Liquid Bomb' terrorists who we have to thank for not being able to take more than 100ml of fluids onto flights any more.

'*What people don't understand is I don't care about the client, and I certainly don't identify with their opinions and actions, but if you surrender legal standards because you don't like the person in the dock, then you are surrendering something that protects you, me and our children, protections that we may want someday for somebody precious to us, and we won't want shortcuts taken then . . .*' It is inarguable logic, but it takes a brave person to make those arguments in relation to some of the most hated people on the planet, and it doesn't come without personal cost. *'Yes, it doesn't always make you popular,'* is her modest way of putting it. *'But you don't tackle terrorism by destroying the law and undermining democracy.'*

In more recent times, even though Helena is a Labour appointee to the House of Lords, she has felt a continual need to hold even her own government to account for potential infringements on our civil liberties. *'I was very critical of what happened in the Blair years. In the 1990s, we'd been moving to a really positive place in terms of human rights, and then after 9/11 we had the business of rounding people up and having detention without trial, extraordinary renditions, the growth of the use of torture and trying to take away trial by jury. It's the responsibility of people like me to speak out about it.'* She pauses for a sip of her tea and states categorically, *'My master is the law, not politics.'*

Those shifting sands in human rights and due process illustrate an uncomfortable truth about civil liberties and politics that has been true throughout history. *'When it comes to human rights they are never permanent, they are like the tide, they come to the fore and they recede. Those who are powerful almost invariably want to hold that power to themselves, so we have to remain eternally vigilant. But when you defend such principles you have to be prepared for a whole section of people to be pissed off at you.'*

I tell her I'm interested in where her resilience comes from, to not shirk such responsibilities when most people do. She gives a deep and profound answer, which, as a new father of a baby girl, means I go home and cuddle my daughter even more than usual. *'I had a father who loved me, who had no difficulty in expressing his love for me. I felt cherished, I felt beloved, I felt confident, and it meant that I was never fearful, so I stepped into the world bold and brave. Women who have that bond with their father are women who are able to do things with their lives or conquer the world.'*

It prompts me to share my belief and hope that my daughter has been born into what will increasingly be a woman's world. Helena agrees, but only to a certain point.

'We've certainly seen huge changes in gender equality, not least because there has been a new generation of men who are more engaged in their children and who don't believe all parenting should be left to the missus, but ultimately it depends on which end of a woman's experience you come in at. If you're a woman in Northern Iraq or the Congo it isn't so good, life is still pretty bloody.'

Which is an answer that makes mincemeat of my naively simplistic assertion.

What is remarkable about Helena is the absolute congruency between her personal beliefs and her actions. It is one thing to believe in equality and human rights, it's another to spend your life fighting for them, and it matches entirely with the philosophy she imparts as her most valuable piece of advice:

> **'Treat everybody as equal value, irrespective of his or her status or who they are. That's the thing I want for my children, I want them to always feel that nobody's better than you and vice versa. That's what my parents taught me. Never treat anybody as lesser and never accept anyone treating you as lesser. Respect the humanness of the other person.'**

And don't forget to tell your kids you love them.

❖

LORD WAHEED ALLI,
CHAMPION OF GENTLEMEN

I'M IN THE OFFICE OF Lord Waheed, one of the UK's most successful media entrepreneurs (*The Word, The Big Breakfast* and *Survivor* all made it to our screens, thanks to him), the first openly gay member of the House of Lords and, of greatest significance, one of the country's most prolific gay rights champions.

His is no ordinary office. It is gloriously sybaritic. We're sitting in armchairs so plump and soft they warrant stroking, fresh herbal tea is being served from a table upon which Lord Alli's trainer-clad feet rest, and the walls are covered entirely with oil paintings, which, on closer inspection, are exclusively of regal-looking young men from a wing-collared past.

I tell Lord Alli that I assume the oil paintings are of some distant ancestors.

'No, nothing like that. It was my fiftieth birthday recently and I told all my friends and family I wanted pictures of handsome eighteenth-century men. Some people like looking at flowers. I like looking at men. So I thought I'd cover my walls with pictures of them.' I shouldn't be surprised by the candour of his answer. As Lord Alli made clear

when he spoke during the debate in the House of Lords on reducing the age of consent for gay sex, *'I have never been confused by my sexuality. I have only ever been confused by people's reactions to it.'*

It's hard to exaggerate how much has changed in the world of gay rights since Tony Blair appointed Lord Alli to the House of Lords as its youngest ever member. From the outset Lord Alli committed to doing everything he could to improve rights for gay people. It started with equality in the age of consent for gay sex, and then each year a new initiative: to repeal Section 28 (that banned literature about homosexuality from schools), to get same-sex parents adoption rights, legislation to prevent discrimination against homosexuals in goods and services, civil unions, gay marriage, the right to marry in religious buildings.

When one looks at his business achievements and then these political achievements, it's a stunningly successful scorecard. And all this from a working-class kid, born to two immigrant parents, who had to leave state school at sixteen to get a job in order to help keep his family fed after his dad walked out on his mum. The definitive self-made man.

So how did he do it?

> *'Well, it starts with the usual stuff that you hear: work hard, be lucky. No one is successful without those two things. But the most important thing of all is maintenance of aim. If I could pass on one thing, it is that. My business success came from maintenance of aim. I said to myself, no matter what else I will make the best programmes I*

can. My political life: maintenance of aim again – get equality for gay rights, no matter what else was going on in my life. And that's what it's about, fight the distractions, keep coming back to your thing, the thing that's most important to you.'

We both reflected on that for a moment. And then he went further.

'*You know, when I was younger being gay was still treated as something to be ashamed of. It meant you had to conduct relationships in secret. It made it more difficult to have sex. I wanted equality so no one had to be ashamed. I wanted to make it easier for people to have sex. I like sex. I think people should be able to have as much sex as they want.'*

Maintenance of aim, right there.

'THE MOST IMPORTANT THING OF ALL IS MAINTENANCE OF AIM. IF I COULD PASS ON ONE THING, IT IS THAT. MY BUSINESS SUCCESS CAME FROM MAINTENANCE OF AIM. I SAID TO MYSELF, NO MATTER WHAT ELSE I WILL MAKE THE BEST PROGRAMMES I CAN. MY POLITICAL LIFE:

MAINTENANCE OF AIM AGAIN —
GET EQUALITY FOR GAY RIGHTS,
NO MATTER WHAT ELSE WAS
GOING ON IN MY LIFE. AND
THAT'S WHAT IT'S ABOUT, FIGHT
THE DISTRACTIONS, KEEP
COMING BACK TO YOUR THING,
THE THING THAT'S MOST
IMPORTANT TO YOU.'

—Lord Waheed Alli

OLIVIA COLMAN CLEANS UP

Olivia Colman, described by Meryl Streep as 'divinely gifted' and one of the most loved and in-demand actresses of her generation, is telling me about her big break. I just assume she's referring to landing her first part, but it turns out she's explaining how she got her first cleaning job, the work she relied on while trying to make it in acting. *'When I was younger, me and my mum were staying at a guesthouse in Cambridge. (We were regulars because it was near the hospital where my dad was.) One day the owner came over and said she wanted to go away for the weekend and that I seemed dependable and looked like I needed some money, so she was going to leave me in charge to clean the rooms and run the place. And I did, and it was lovely.'*

It's certainly not the path-to-stardom story I was expecting, but Olivia seems as proud of her cleaning reviews as the ones she gets for her acting. *'I was a very good cleaner, people said so. I really enjoyed the job. And I was very honest. If anyone had a secret camera, they'd know I never looked in drawers.'*

This modesty and self-deprecation is typical of Olivia. When we chat, she jokingly asks me to write that she's thinner and taller in real life, which of course she is, and she has a weapons' grade loveliness about her. In person you get hit first by her disarmingly sweet, warm smile, at odds with the naughty words that sometimes come out of her lips but entirely congruent with the personality beneath. She even has a daily ritual for bringing that loveliness to life: *'I have a little rule which I've had for about twenty years now. When I leave my front door in the morning, I'm not allowed back in till I've done something nice for someone. It makes you feel nice and helps you remember you're lucky.'*

Maybe those random acts of kindness are payback for something her schoolteacher did for her. Olivia had never thought of acting, but her English teacher persuaded her to audition for the school play when she was sixteen. Suffice to say, she loved it. *'That first experience of people clapping and laughing, fucking brilliant. It was like a first try of drugs or something, it was my heroin. And I thought if only I could earn my keep doing this it would be amazing.'*

Back then, she just assumed it was impossible. *'My mum was a nurse, my dad a surveyor, I just assumed it was a silly dream and wouldn't happen, but the older I got, the more terrible I realised I was at everything else and that sort of helped, it meant I couldn't resort to something else.'* Olivia lists the other jobs she tried to do. *'I was an awful teacher, there's a generation of children that had a lucky escape. Then I learned to type but was a terrible secretary. Thank God for the cleaning, otherwise I would have starved.'*

Unlike with the cleaning, she says there was no big break in acting, *'it's been more of a slow sizzle really'*. The first five years were tough, constantly auditioning, not getting parts. But, she says, *'It's a good thing I spent years not working, I appreciate it so much more. I hear some stories about actors behaving badly on set and they don't realise how fucking lucky they are. I want to work with them just so I can have a word.'* I have no doubt she would.

These days there's a bit less cleaning going on. She's so much in demand, directors even change parts so Olivia can play them. In the recent TV production of John le Carré's *The Night Manager*, Olivia's spy character was originally a man but the production had the part rewritten as female. And then Olivia happily found out before the audition she was going to have a third baby, so they rewrote the character again to match Olivia at the time of filming: six months' pregnant.

I say it's a sign of how much she was wanted that they changed the spy character to a woman. As usual, she bats the praise away and says it is more a reflection of society moving on and it no longer being acceptable to have all male casts. What about them rewriting the part again to accommodate her unborn baby? *'Well, spies get pregnant, too.'*

Given her constant refusal to take credit and her twin hallmarks of being totally grounded and lovely, her advice comes as no real surprise.

> **'If you're ever lucky enough to be successful in what you choose to do, don't ever believe your own hype, and remember it could all stop tomorrow. Do whatever you do to the best of your ability. Take the job seriously, but not yourself. And most of all, be nice to work with.'**

And if you need some help with the housework, you know who to call.

'Spies get

pregnant, too.'

– OLIVIA COLMAN

THE ENDURING JAMES RHODES

THE FIRST TIME I HEARD the concert pianist James Rhodes play I didn't know who he was. The occasion wasn't even a musical event, more a theatrical evening celebrating letters of note. But on stage was a grand piano, and as the house lights went down, a skinny, scruffy man in black jeans and beaten trainers shuffled, eyes down, over to the piano and crumpled himself over the keys under a tangle of bed-head hair. Blimey, I remember thinking to myself, he doesn't look like much of a concert pianist. I suspect most of the audience was thinking the same. But a few seconds after he started playing we were all thinking something different, and a few mesmerising seconds after that we weren't thinking anything at all.

Many people say that music has changed their life, but in James's case it literally saved his. When James was in his twenties and sectioned in a psychiatric hospital, he was found hanging by his neck from the noose he'd fashioned out of a TV aerial cable in an enterprising and determined effort to kill himself. At his very lowest ebb following this failed suicide, a thoughtful friend smuggled into his room an iPod loaded with the *Goldberg Variations* inside a bottle of shampoo. Listening to that music gave James a respite from the demons and reminded him there may be some things worth staying alive for after all.

The reason why James tied himself to that cable was ultimately due to the brutal rape he suffered by his gym teacher every week from the age of five to ten, an ordeal so repeated and extreme it left him with spinal and intestinal issues, as well as deeper, more insidious mental traumas. He is therefore a man to be congratulated not just for his musical mastery (called a 'genuinely poetic gift' by *The Independent*) but also for the more profound achievement of enduring those internal onslaughts to stay alive.

The other thing to say about James is he is also very funny. When we hook up in Starbucks for the first time and I proclaim it's good to meet him in person after all our texts and emails, he responds in a hushed voice, *'Fucking hell, mate, keep your voice down, people will think we're on a Tinder date.'* And he gives great conversation, although, with his language, you wouldn't want your mother listening.

I tell him he completely transformed the whole room the time I heard him play, but he is having none of it: he left feeling angry with his performance. He says the perfectionist in him always does. *'I can think I fucked it because on one note out of ten thousand I put four grams too much pressure on the key and it should have been a tiny micro decibel quieter but wasn't.'* Such are the obsessiveness and high standards he applies in pursuit of the impossible: the perfect performance. But he's not complaining. *'Music is the one enhancer in life that doesn't have shitty side effects and doesn't cost a fortune, and I have the opportunity to surround myself in it every day. It's almost too good to be true. But it is true, so I know how lucky I am.'*

His approach to classical music is deeply respectful to the composers while being refreshingly anarchic towards the industry. As likely to be playing the main stage at summer festivals as the Royal Albert Hall, he interjects performances with personal anecdotes about the composers and releases albums with bad boy titles like *Bullets and Lullabies* and *Razor Blades, Small Pills and Big Pianos*. He is an insurgent on a mission to get Bach and Beethoven to the masses, or die trying.

James originally discovered the piano as a place of refuge during the early years of his secret childhood torture, but after opting for university instead of music college he gave up the piano at eighteen and didn't touch it for ten years. Tellingly, that decade without playing was when his *'twitching, itching head gremlins'* did the most damage, culminating in the suicide attempt. But that iPod moment in treatment restored his resolve to at least get into the music industry. He set himself the goal of becoming an agent for classical pianists and contacted a well-respected agent to ask for a job. At the interview, the agent got him to play the piano. The agent listened for fifteen minutes and said he would not support James being an agent, he *had* to become a performer instead. And the rest of the story is coming to a cinema near you soon (his autobiography, *Instrumental*, is being turned into a movie).

I congratulate him on his success and also for the discipline he manages in his life as a concert pianist, getting up each morning to practise all day, every day. The ferocity of his response surprises me.

'That's not discipline, I love to practise. Discipline is showing up to work on time, doing the commute, paying your mortgage, getting your

kids dressed, feeding them and packing them off to school. That's discipline. That's endurance. And it's the most underrated, invisible, heroic fucking thing, just to fucking get through a day without reward or applause when all you want to do is fucking punch yourself in the face and throw yourself off a building.'

Essentially, he is a man living his dream while still having to endure the nightmare. 'Look, I know how good my life looks. I'm privileged to do what I do. But I still want to die more often than I want to live, and I know I am only some meds and a couple of weeks from being back in that psychiatric ward.'

Given he knows about living with demons better than most, I ask his advice for anyone currently in the depths of a trauma themselves.

> **'Well, you can say all the normal things like talk to people, look after yourself, ask for help. But none of that makes any difference. It makes no difference at all. I guess my advice is, and it's not really advice, it's more a wish: I wish that you're lucky enough to survive when you don't want to, because things can get better. Just survive. Just survive any way you can.'** ∗

∗ If you're suffering, please consider contacting Mind, a leading mental-health charity. They will provide support and generally fight your corner. Visit their website for more information: www.mind.org.uk.

'Just survive.
Just survive anyway
you can.'

— *James Rhodes*

THE FEARLESS
RIGHT REVEREND LIBBY LANE

R ELIGION, IT'S A MAN'S WORLD. Or at least historically it has been. But I am sitting with the person who best illustrates the Church of England's commitment to begin changing that: the Bishop of Stockport, also known as the Right Reverend Libby Lane, the first-ever female bishop in the UK.

'It wasn't about me. It was a moment of change and I just happened to be in it,' is Bishop Lane's take on her involvement in arguably the most significant development in the history of the Church of England since its inception. Her modesty is genuine. She never sought to be made a bishop, her Church elders asked her. So she answered the call, but would no more take credit for this quiet revolutionary moment than she would renounce Jesus and partner up with the Devil.

Like most upsets to the status quo, her ordination met with resistance, right up to and including the actual consecration, where some of her fellow bishops refused to lay their hands upon her and a priest shouted out his objections from the congregation and in front of a live TV audience. I ask her opinion of such senior Church members, who were and still are against female bishops. *'I think they're wrong, but I don't doubt they are Godly and Christian people, and the institution is right to have allowed them to hold that place because God is bigger than all of us.'* Libby pauses, and then adds, with a touch more revolutionary spirit, *'Come judgement day, it might turn out they were right and I shouldn't be doing this, but I can live with that.'*

It turns out that flash of constructive independence, defiance even, is not a one-off but a recurring aspect of Libby's character. And it started early. Libby was first introduced to Church aged eleven by a friend, as her family did not attend, and she became so deeply involved in the Church her excesses, praying rather than partying, were not typical of a teenage girl. *'I wasn't consciously rebelling but establishing an independent identity, as you need to do as a teenager. And I feel blessed I was able to do it with something that has been so constructive and life-affirming and positive.'*

Her commitment came not from feeling the hand of God when she first walked into church, but simply from being accepted and acknowledged by her fellow church goers. *'They treated me as an equal from the beginning. I was not just an eleven-year-old girl, I was me. The minister remembered my name and that small thing as an indication of consideration for me as a child was significant.'*

These young years spent in the Church and among its congregation allowed for a deeper, longer-lasting sense of purpose and faith to develop. *'The community was such a gift to me. It was a safe place to discover that we are all interdependent, and we are responsible not only to God but to one another. I learnt I could put others before myself because I in turn was being looked after by others, and that by being prepared to let go and prioritise others, I was in turn held and treasured.'*

I spend over two hours talking religion with Libby Lane. We cover every topic imaginable in relation to her faith, her God, her Church, its failings and its teachings. I've never met anyone so gentle in spirit yet so firm in resolve. So open to challenge yet so steadfast in belief. So clear-sighted about the issues of her organisation, yet so enamoured of its fundamental principles. Her level of inner peace and reassurance is unlike anyone else's I have encountered. To put it crassly, one is left with a sense of *'I want some of what she's having'*.

In a particularly still and significant moment, Libby shares the most deeply held belief underpinning her life, identity, career and faith, and the resulting sense of peace: she, like all of us, is loved by God. *'What comes first is God's regard for us, and that gives a sense of self-regard that doesn't need to be generated or sought from external events. It means I am free and at peace and have purpose and hope.'* Such is the absolute nature of this belief it gave her the confidence to follow her calling into the Church, even though at that time there were no signs women would ever be ordained. And then to endure the pain of being ostracised by some of the elders of her revered institution when it finally became possible. She did it all simply because, as she puts it, *'I could do no other.'*

This deep sense of belonging, of reassurance, that religion can bring is inextricably contained within her answer when I ask for her most valuable piece of advice:

❖

'IT IS A CONSTANT REFRAIN
IN SCRIPTURE: "DO NOT BE
AFRAID" — DON'T LIVE OUT OF
FEAR. OF COURSE, IT IS
NATURAL THAT WE ALL
SOMETIMES FEEL AFRAID.
WE'RE AFRAID OF BEING
ALONE, OF FAILING, OF NOT
COPING. BUT IF WE LIVE OUR
LIVES FROM A PLACE OF FEAR,
IT IS DAMAGING TO US, TO
OUR RELATIONSHIPS, TO OUR
COMMUNITIES. ONE NEEDS TO

FIND SOMETHING THAT GIVES A SENSE OF SAFETY, OF SECURITY, OF HOME. AND THAT COMES WITH ACCEPTING WE ARE ALL KNOWN BY GOD AND LOVED BY GOD. IF YOU ALLOW THAT TRUTH IN, IT ENABLES YOU TO FIND FREEDOM FROM FEAR. SO YOU CAN LIVE OUT NOT OF FEAR BUT OF HOPE AND GRATITUDE.'

– The Right Reverend Libby Lane

ALAIN DE BOTTON,
GHOST HUNTER

A S I HEAD THROUGH THE baggage area of Heathrow Airport my thoughts turn, as they always do at this point in a journey, to Alain de Botton, the writer and philosopher of everyday life. In his book *A Week at the Airport* (the title is literal, he penned the book over seven days of living, sleeping and writing in Heathrow's Terminal 5), he describes the irrational optimism and subsequent sadness we all experience when we pass through the doors into the arrivals area and secretly scan the faces and signs of the people waiting, hoping there might be someone there for us, even though we know no one is coming. Until reading that, I thought it was just me.

It's one of a thousand examples of what the man does best: sifting through and observing, grain by grain, the fragile sand castle of the human psyche, and reassuring us that the kaleidoscope of thoughts and emotions we each experience on a typical day is normal and it doesn't make us mad. Or, at least, no more so than the next person.

His North London home, where we meet, is a physical manifestation of his work. It's located on a quiet street between an old church and a painter's studio, a place of philosophical respite between the worlds of art and religion, two of the many subjects he writes on. And the quiet garden room we sit in is primed for therapeutic enquiry – two comfy chairs face one another inviting conversation, a box of tissues and day-bed are on hand in case matters become too troubling, and a wall of books lends a re-assuringly informed air to the proceedings.

Alain de Botton's output is prolific: thirteen books covering art, sex, work, relationships, travel, religion and the other big topics life is made of. On top of that he has presented countless documentaries and set up a learning centre called the School of Life, which runs courses on coping with the various dilemmas that come with being human. Alain de Botton is, without a doubt, a philosopher on a mission: *'My goal is a more emotionally literate, happier society, but one that doesn't in any way overlook the fact that life is tragic in structure.'*

One of his main beliefs is that most people assume the big problems in society are political and economic, and we down-play the significance of emotions because they are *'seen as somehow not quite serious, they're something you do at the weekend, but the more serious-sounding things like economics and politics are really, for the most part, about human emotions and human emotional functioning'*.

Furthermore, it is often our emotional selves that *'cause the problems of addiction, relationship breakdown, anxiety, anger, frustration, all the other day-to-day miseries that hold people back'*. And given the scale of the problems, it struck him as strange that there wasn't a single academic discipline that prepares you *'for what it means* to be an emotional creature that's, a lot of the time, slightly out of control'. Hence his life's work of finding ways for us to guide and console ourselves.

So was this always his calling? Did he set out from an early age to help navigate the human condition?

'Look, I'm a timid, obedient soul by nature. I wanted to have a normal job. I was a swot, I liked obeying orders, I liked to fit in. But I knew it was all fake, I knew it was all rubbish. I was just doing it to please my very demanding family and to be a good chap, but as I grew older, the idea of a normal job, of being a management accountant or whatever, increasingly made me feel dead inside. But it left me with a crisis as I left university, thinking, so what now?'

His view is that society places a lot of pressure on people to know what they want to do and that pressure can be disabling. While some lucky people *do* know from an early age what they want to do, and others are happy just to do a job if it pays the bills, there is a large third category of people who feel, *'I know there's something I want to do, but I don't know what it is yet. And the world can be quite impatient with those people. Unless you can say to the world "I want to do a specific thing", we're steamrollered.'*

So Alain de Botton's advice on how to lead a more nourishing life speaks directly to those people in that third category: *'Find the thing that drives you. It's not easy. Most of us are not obvious to ourselves. But we occasionally pick up indistinct signals, some kind of vague longing, from something that feels like a ghost-self, deep within us, something that refuses to die but is not quite alive either. That ghost is our true self, trying to come out. Listen out for it. We have to turn our ghost-self into a real person. We need to bring the ghost to life.'*

I ask for tips for those people trying to track down their ghost. Surprisingly, envy, pessimism and death are all to be enlisted to help with the ghost hunt.

'Analyse what you are envious of. It is very unlikely we actually envy a whole person, if you break it down you'll find you actually just envy specific attributes of them, say their approach to graphic design or their ability to make cakes, and you can build up, from an analysis of your envy, a model of your ideal self.'

You'll also need to experiment and try new things, so a background pessimism helps take the pressure off. *'"It's all going to go wrong" is a useful starting point, allowing us to make peace with failure. I've calmed myself down in risky ventures many times with a sense of "Oh fuck it, it may all blow up, but that's OK."'*

Finally, you can use death to help, albeit indirectly. *'One doesn't want to frighten people but, obviously, life is extremely short and reminding ourselves of that should invigorate us and shake us from a kind of lethargy when we are searching.'*

And if after all that you still don't know what to do, then don't worry. Alain says it could be that the angst-ridden, existential philosophers of the mid-twentieth century were right all along. They believed we're all shooting in the dark when it comes to making the big decisions about what to do with our lives and we shouldn't expect to know, or even enjoy finding out. Ultimately they just accepted the wisdom of Solon instead, who decreed: Let no man be called happy before his death.

Cheery lot, these philosophers.

'WE HAVE TO TURN
OUR GHOST-SELF INTO
A REAL PERSON. WE NEED
TO BRING THE GHOST
TO LIFE.'

– Alain de Botton

RUBY WAX'S FUNNY MIND

'*I couldn't stop. I was even doing gags during my Caesarean.*' Ruby Wax, actress, writer and comedian, is recounting the unhealthy pressure she used to feel to be funny. She's not complaining, just explaining one of the downsides of being a professional comedian: the expectation that you'll always clown around and be amusing.

What compounded the pressure to be funny was Ruby's history of heavy bouts of depression, a reality she felt she had to deny, given her day job. This hiding of her illness even reached its logical extreme – she once discharged herself from a mental treatment centre where she was a patient to go interview someone for a TV show, then returned to the hospital that evening. '*When I got back the inmates looked at me and said, "Are you crazy?" Which was high praise coming from them.*'

She is still a very funny lady, but she has a second, more serious focus these days: campaigning for greater mental health and de-stigmatising the issue. It's an area she knows a lot about, not just from her own experiences but also because in a bid to understand the illness that would periodically floor her she did a Masters in mindfulness-based cognitive behavioural therapy at

Oxford and made it her mission to unpick what was going on when depression strikes.

She didn't intend for this new path to make her a poster child for mental health, but she became one, quite literally. A Comic Relief-funded initiative to promote awareness of mental illness placed posters all over the London Underground which featured Ruby saying she'd experienced depression. She was originally shocked by the attention: *'I thought it looked like a showbiz poster, but I decided to piggyback on it by writing a show on mental illness and pretending that I did the whole thing on purpose.'* She performed the show for the first time in The Priory treatment clinic, where she had previously recovered from a breakdown, and because it was so well received it toured round other mental health institutes throughout the country. Books and more shows followed, each with a purpose of providing respite, insight and counsel for people with the anxieties and issues of the modern-day mind.

After twenty-five years of making people laugh on telly, she says these days she would rather be in the smoking room of mental institutes talking to the patients she now refers to as *'my people'*. And while it would be difficult to think of anyone who has done more to get mental health issues out into the open, she's not done yet. Her latest initiative is to roll out Frazzled Cafés, walk-in meetings held at M&S stores across the country where people who are on *'the cusp of burning out, who are feeling isolated'* can meet up, support each other and share stories.

It all fits with Ruby's gloriously open-minded, open-hearted approach to mental illness: get it out in the open, get it talked about. Stop suffering it in silence and feeling like you have to hide it. She knows there are no easy solutions, and while she advocates daily exercises of mindfulness (*'you have to practise, you don't get a six pack just by thinking about one'*) she's also pragmatic about taking meds if they work for you: *'If you were a diabetic, you would take the insulin.'*

She does still get hit with depression sometimes, the difference being it now lasts weeks rather than months, and she is better at noticing it and dealing with it. In terms of the advice she gives, it neither downplays nor overstates the significance of how you respond to the mental illness.

> *'Don't get depressed about the depression. Depression can bring with it a sense of shame, that we beat ourselves up for having it, that we're ashamed to have this vulnerability. But you have to forgive yourself and allow yourself to feel it. It's normal and it's natural and a basic human foible that affects one in four of us. Take strength and solidarity from those numbers.'*

IN THE DARK
WITH SHEP GORDON

W E'RE ON A CRUISE SHIP out of Miami. It's midnight.
There's more than 3,000 entrepreneurs on board.
It's billed as a seminar-at-sea; in reality, it's a party
weekend thinly disguised as a conference. But most of us, for once,
are forgoing the bars and clubs and restaurants. Instead, we're packed
into the main auditorium, listening reverently to one man in shorts,
sandals and a Bermuda shirt talk on stage. That man is Shep Gordon.

There are only two types of people in the world: those who
love Shep Gordon and those who don't know who he is. For
those in the second camp, the best place to start is *Supermensch:
The Legend of Shep Gordon*, the documentary made by his friend
Mike Myers. It covers the life and times of one of the most loved
men and managers in Hollywood, who started his career master-
minding the infamous reputation of Alice Cooper in the 1970s,
and who now acts as close advisor to the Dali Lama, via pretty
much everyone else of note.

The documentary is a masterclass in hedonism, friendship, drug
consumption, management and spirituality. It seems no one has
led a faster life, a fuller life, a life more dedicated to making other

people happy. The documentary is like watching a video made for a loved one's milestone birthday, but rather than it being their family members expressing their love and telling naughty stories, it is every Hollywood star you can think of.

I caught Shep after his speech, which had been peppered with anecdote after anecdote of eye-raising excess, profound Buddhist insights and brilliant juicy gossip. And Shep, through it all, came across as a man who is at peace with himself. Who is happy. Who is doing what he wants to do. He says as much when passing on his advice.

'My advice is follow your bliss.'

I ask him to expand.

'If you want to have a good life, you have to find out, and then only do, what makes you happy.'

And if you don't know what that is?

'Then my advice is this – go into a room, a dark room, by yourself, for at least thirty minutes every day. And sit there in the dark and think. And keep doing that, keep going into that room every day, until you have worked out what it is that makes you happy.'

I asked him, other than sitting in dark rooms, what is his bliss.

'My bliss is making other people happy. I've been trying to do that all my life.'

An answer that chimed with everything we had seen and heard. As did his final comment.

'*And now I am going to make myself happy by going back to my cabin, sitting on my balcony and rolling myself a nice big spliff.*'
Shep Gordon: Supermensch.

'FOLLOW YOUR BLISS.
IF YOU WANT TO HAVE
A GOOD LIFE, YOU HAVE
TO FIND OUT, AND THEN
ONLY DO, WHAT MAKES
YOU HAPPY.'

– *Shep Gordon*

THE TEENAGE BRAINS OF
PROFESSOR SARAH-JAYNE
BLAKEMORE

I T'S RARE TO MEET SOMEONE who really knows what they're talking about, but Dr Sarah-Jayne Blakemore, Professor of Cognitive Neuroscience at UCL, is such a person. Her chosen specialised subject is the teenage brain, and few people know more about it than her.

Sarah-Jayne has researched teenagers and their neurological activities for the last fifteen years. As evidence of how front-edge Dr Blakemore's work has been, when she originally applied for grants to examine the adolescent brain she was rejected because the grant-makers said it was not even an area of research. Simply put, virtually no one had actually ever investigated the teenage neurological years. Sarah-Jayne helped to change all that.

It was natural scientific curiosity that led Professor Blakemore to first embark on her journey into the teenage mind. Originally, her area of research was schizophrenia. After studying hundreds of patients, she noticed that every patient said their symptoms had started between the ages of eighteen and twenty-six. So she became intrigued by what was happening to the brain in the years just before the issues materialised. When she searched for information on the teenage brain, however, the cupboard was almost bare. So she decided to study teenagers herself.

It is such endeavour that has turned the general consensus on teenage neurology – that the brain stops developing in childhood and nothing much changes after that – on its head. What Sarah-Jayne and her colleagues showed by studying willing teenagers in MRI brain-scanning machines is that the brain in adolescent years undergoes huge developments, and these changes help to explain some of the behaviours associated with teenage years: the risk-taking, being influenced by peers, self-consciousness. Furthermore, these adaptive behaviours that are often dismissed as 'hormonal' or moody, serve a fundamental and evolutionary purpose. Teenagers need to take those risks and be influenced by others in order to develop a sense of self-identity and to become independent from their parents. And the continuing investigations into adolescent brains are starting to unravel the neurological drivers behind such teenage mental health issues as eating disorders, anxiety and depression, making the right solutions more likely to be found.

Sarah-Jayne's work has heightened her empathy for her subjects, and she hopes it will do the same for society. *'My research has totally changed my view of teenagers. I now feel like such an advocate for them, as they are a sector of society that gets so much shit, we just kind of write them off, make fun of them. They are the only group in society it is still OK to stigmatise. I can't tell you how many people I've met who, when I say I study the teenage brain, say, "I didn't think teenagers had brains." We wouldn't accept that talk of any other part of society.'*

So, given her greater understanding of the inner lives of teen-agers, I ask her advice on how best to handle someone going through those difficult adolescent years:

> *'The important thing is to cut them some slack: at fifteen they may look like an adult, but they don't have the brains of one, so make allowances for them. And don't write them off. At any point. Someone who is showing no aptitude for learning could still come good: their brain is going to keep on developing, and what is a sieve today could be a sponge tomorrow. Allow them time and space for their brain to do its thing. Don't hurry them. Their adult brains will thank you.'*

WINNING WITH
LAWRENCE DALLAGLIO

'*L*osing is disgusting. There is absolutely nothing good about losing at all. If you play sport at the level I did, you have to hate losing. It has to make you feel physically ill.'

I'm not going to argue, not least because you don't argue with a man the size of Lawrence Dallaglio, former England Rugby Captain and the only team member to play in every single minute of their 2003 Rugby World Cup-winning campaign. The man is a *unit*.

We're talking about what it takes to achieve mastery and dominance in your chosen sport. And given that he is the most capped and longest playing professional rugby player the UK has ever seen, he knows what he is talking about.

Dallaglio admits talent is important, but it's not the main thing: '*you can add talent on later if you have an unquenchable thirst for learning new things, for practicing over and over and over again*'. He talks about the unglamorous reality of the professional sports player; the repetitiveness of perfecting that touch, that kick, that pass. All day, every day.

He is clear that winning comes easy to nobody, especially not the people who make it look easy. *'You have to suffer for it. And every time you go onto the pitch there is another team that needs to win and hates to lose just as much as you do. They want to destroy all your hard work. They want to take it away from you.'*

So how do you face the pressure of playing at that level and make sure you leave the pitch as the team carrying the trophy?

In the final analysis, Dallaglio explains that winning or losing begins and ends with what's inside your head. If it's about anything, it is about self-belief. It is the doubts as well as the techniques that professionals have to master.

> **'You start the week thinking: we have to play the All Blacks on Saturday, how the hell are we going to beat them? But beating them is your job. So you have to sit yourself down and tell yourself whatever you have to tell yourself so you start to believe it, that you can beat them, that you WILL beat them. You may even have to lie a bit to yourself at first to get the belief going. Whatever it takes. And from then on, once you start to believe, you make sure you're searingly honest with yourself. Are you working as hard as you could? Have you done everything, and I mean everything, you can to get ready for that match? And the answer always has to be yes. There has to be no doubt in your mind. Otherwise, you're going to lose.'**

And we know how much he doesn't want to do that. Lawrence Dallaglio: most definitely not a loser.

'ARE YOU WORKING AS HARD AS YOU COULD? HAVE YOU DONE EVERYTHING, AND I MEAN EVERYTHING, YOU CAN TO GET READY FOR THAT MATCH? AND THE ANSWER ALWAYS HAS TO BE YES.'

— Lawrence Dallaglio

MARGARET BUSBY,
DAUGHTER OF AFRICA

I'M GETTING THE INSIDE SCOOP on creating your own publishing company from Margaret Busby, writer, broadcaster, literary critic and co-founder of Allison & Busby, a bold and rule-breaking publisher started in the 1960s. *'We had no money and didn't know what we were doing,'* she says of herself and Clive Allison. *'All we had were our ideals and a lot of energy.'*

Those ideals and energy were evident from the very first book they published. It was a Black Power novel called *The Spook Who Sat by the Door*, about an African-American spy in the CIA who realises he has been recruited as a 'token black' and goes rogue, recruiting young black 'freedom fighters' to rebel against the government. In the racially charged atmosphere of the late 1960s, the novel was considered too controversial and had been turned down by every house on either side of the Atlantic. But Margaret believed in the writer and the importance of the story, so she borrowed £50 to house the author in London and worked with him on the manuscript.

'When it was done we sent it to The Observer *suggesting they serialise it, and they sent it back saying that they didn't serialise fiction*

and even if they did it wouldn't be a Black Power first novel like this. We sent it back to them saying "You're wrong" and they ended up running it.'

Margaret's commitment to using the written word to tell important stories and give voice to unheard people is a constant over her five-decades-long career. The mission of her company was *'to do the things that nobody else was doing that we thought should be done'*. Along with publishing authors of all creed, colour and nationality, she made literary history with her magnum opus, *Daughters of Africa,* a thousand-page collection of words and writing from more than two hundred women of African descent, celebrated for giving a global platform to their overlooked, forgotten and underrated voices.

Her understanding of what it is to be marginalised is personal. Not just from being a Ghana-born child sent to be educated in English boarding schools, but as a black woman working in what was back then a publishing industry dominated by white men. She constantly encountered an ingrained low-level racism, where people who came across her company just assumed that her white male business partner, Allison, was in charge, and she, as the black woman, was his assistant, or lover, or both. *'Society's view was that I was not equal. Everyone from the bank manager to the window cleaner would always ask to speak to my partner. I was just the black girl.'*

In a different form, she's still on the receiving end of such assumptions today. *'I only get asked to review books by black people. I went to university, I studied English, I know Shakespeare, but all I get asked to cover is black literature.'* She says it's *'not because people are bigoted, just unimaginative'*.

I ask her if it bothers her. *'I once did say to an editor, "You know, I can also review white writers." And then the work dried up. They were too embarrassed to send me black writers, but they still didn't send me white ones.'*

There's no air of defeat or complaint from Margaret, just a straightforward chronicling of what it is to be a black woman in a white man's world. *'I could have a fight every single day, but sometimes you're better off to just bite your tongue and move on.'*

In an obtuse way, there are similarities between being a publisher and an editor, where a certain amount of tongue-biting is necessary. *'Your job is to edit a writer and if you do it well, people say what a wonderful author, but if the book is bad they say what a terrible editor. But that's par for the course.'* She likens the role to being *'sort of a midwife. You help the writer say what they want to say in the best way possible. You can't have an ego.'*

Interestingly, her main hobby mirrors her career of making sure stories are told and voices are heard – and being happy to miss out on the credit for doing so. She anonymously writes literally hundreds of Wikipedia pages, for anything she regards significant: people, events, publishers, books and music. *'It's important. Otherwise things happen, people die and they're gone, forgotten forever. This way it's a legacy for the future, a tree of sorts.'*

Her two favourite pieces of advice relate to this commitment to making things better without any expectation to reap the benefits. Firstly, she repeats Harry Truman's famous quote: *'It's amazing what you can accomplish if you do not care who takes the credit.'* A suitable mantra for a woman who has worked tirelessly behind the scenes to promote diversity and tackle prejudice across the cultural arts. But she says her approach to life is ultimately best captured by a Greek proverb she read:

> *'A society grows great when old men plant trees under which they know they will never sit.'*

It's a beautiful encapsulation of what she does.

I am pleased to discover when I go online later that someone in society has gone to Wikipedia and planted a tree for Margaret Busby.

'It's amazing what you can accomplish if you do not care who takes the credit.'

— *Harry Truman*
via Margaret Busby

JAMES CORDEN,
MAN OF THE WORLD

E LSTREE FILM STUDIOS IN NORTH London arguably
lacks some of the glamour and pizazz of its Hollywood
equivalents, but on the plus side it does have a local
Nando's. It's also where the eleventh series of *A League of Their
Own* is being recorded, hosted by the UK's hottest acting/
presenting/writing/car-pooling export, James Corden.

I'm shown into his dressing-room in the afternoon before the
evening's show. The TV is on. James is sat on a sofa watching his
mate Andy Murray's Wimbledon semi-final and he invites me to
come join him. We both become transfixed by the game, sitting
side by side, with our feet up on the coffee table, passing the
occasional comment on the match. Then, after a little while, some
Nando's arrives, and I find myself having a TV dinner with the
biggest guy on it right now.

It has to be said, James Corden makes a great TV dinner
companion. He has that indefinable quality where you relax as
soon as you meet him. His talents for singing, acting, writing,
presenting and even dancing would be intimidating in someone
else, but his 'good guy' vibes are even stronger. You instinctively

feel he is in your corner. Or, in this case, corner-sofa.

That easy-going, humble charm is part of the reason why the biggest names in entertainment all want to appear on his internet-breaking US TV show. Adele rode with him in *Carpool Karaoke*, Justin Bieber dressed in James's clothes and co-presented the programme, and Tom Hanks re-enacted nine of his most famous movie scenes with James for the launch episode. Celebrities don't even do it to plug their latest whatevers, they just want to do the show.

No one appreciates America's Triple A-list making him feel so welcome more than James. *'I don't quite know what I've done to deserve such brilliant memories. Just last week I was driving around the White House with Michelle Obama and I thought to myself, "I don't think this would have happened if I'd stayed in High Wycombe."'*

A big factor in the A-list's involvement is that the guests feel safe. They know with James they're not going to end up looking stupid, unless they want to. *'There's a degree of trust that comes from the fact that I am not interested in making anyone do anything but shine. And we always start from what is going to bring the most joy.'*

Joy creation is an apt description for what James does for a living. And for us, the viewer, that joy partly comes from seeing that James himself is loving every second of it. *'I learnt that from my time on Broadway in* The History Boys. *People always said they loved that we looked like we were having a blast, so I thought to myself, if that's what people like then why don't I aim to actually have a good time rather than just act like I am.'*

In fact, enjoying the experience comes relatively easily. *'I just don't remember a time when I didn't want to perform, or, let's be honest, show off in some capacity.'* But the quality of the output requires a serious work ethic. One of the reasons why James loves partnering up with the greats is because it helps to raise his own game. He recounts how Tom Hanks flew in a day early to rehearse with James over and over again for the launch show. *'I just couldn't stop going "Thank you so much for doing this" and he said, "James, this is showbusiness. And showbusiness is about working really hard, because the harder you work, the quicker you can forget about it." And I thought, "Oh my God. You're so right." The things you work hard on and do well, they never play on your mind, it's the ones where you didn't quite give it your all that plague you after.'* A principle that holds true in life generally.

Gavin and Stacey is one of the things James has never had to give another thought to. Every line he and his co-writer Ruth Jones wrote, and the delivery of each one of them, stands the test of time, as evidenced by the *Friends*-esque continual repeats on British satellite TV. I tell him the series to me quietly and brilliantly captures all the beautiful idiosyncrasies and nonsense of being British, and that if an alien species wanted to understand our country you could tell them to just have a cup of tea and watch all twenty episodes.

James slightly pushes back on this and says he hoped the programme was more universal than British; he would *'prefer it if someone said this is a story about people who fell in love and because of that their families changed and then their family's family changed, and that happens all over the world'*. Which highlights another reason for his success: that the content James creates has universal appeal:

Carpool Karaoke is as joyful to people in Iran as it is to people in Iceland or Italy.

This truth that James's success illustrates, that no matter where people are, they find the same jokes funny, the same stories interesting and want to see the same people in front of the camera, informs in him a bigger worldview. *'We're all so much more alike than different. And if you don't necessarily think of yourself as being particular to one country but as a citizen of the world, then so many issues are reduced. For example, you don't think firstly how can we reduce immigration into our country, you instead think how can we make all of our countries better.'*

He tells a sweet story of passing this one-world ethos on to his five-year-old son, who'd asked him recently why it was important to recycle.

'I said, "Imagine if you found a floating ball that's twenty-five foot by twenty-five foot and not only is it floating but it rotates slightly, and if you get closer to it you can see loads of tiny creatures on it walking around. And if you look even more closely, not one of them is the same, they are all completely unique, and they hug each other and love each other and build amazing things. And if then someone came along and went, "Let's just pour some acid on this bit of the ball here, and cover this bit with loads of rubbish," people would be up in arms and say we have to protect this forever, wouldn't they? Well, our Earth is that ball. And he was just like, "Yeah, OK, Dad. Can we go outside and play now?"'

Given that he is passing on wisdom, I ask him for his best piece of advice. In response, he advocates the importance of finding one's 'thing'.

'There is an inner steel that comes from knowing you're good at something. It might be plumbing or building tables or driving a cab or whatever, but being able to say "When it comes to this, I know what I'm doing" is good for one's confidence. So my advice to someone younger is search for the thing you're good at and don't stop.'

After passing on this advice, he then candidly recounts how finding his thing helped him find his inner steel and deal with times he had as a kid getting picked on.

'I remember being at school, thinking, yes, you can run faster than me and you're stronger than me and you're better at maths than me and you're better at playing the piano, but when the school play comes around you're nowhere. And it stopped me feeling too bullied and outcast.'

That sense of self, of having something he was good at, emboldened him. And he finishes by telling me of the time he went to the careers advisor and they asked what he was going to do when he was older. *'I said, "I'm going to be an actor," and they said, "No, you might want to be an actor, but you will need something else." And I just said, "No, I am going to be an actor," and committed myself fully to that. After all, if you don't give up, you'll never fail.'*

It's a commitment that clearly paid off, and us viewers get to enjoy his success just as much as he does.

NICOLA STURGEON,
THE BRAVE

THE SCOTTISH PARLIAMENT IS ON its summer recess, and Nicola Sturgeon, Scotland's First Minister, is about to head off on holiday, destination: Portugal. The First Minister is looking forward to some downtime and has a suitcase full of books so she can indulge in her favourite form of relaxation, but as holiday locations go it is her second choice, selected because her husband's family has a place out there. So what would her first choice be? Well, that should come as no surprise: Scotland.

Nicola Sturgeon is the essence of Scotland manifested in a person, a political Braveheart destined to lead her beloved country to independence or to die trying. She has turned the electoral map of Scotland yellow, the colour of the Scottish National Party, a party she joined as a student, aged sixteen, and became leader of at forty-four. In 2015 she fought her first general election as both leader of her party and as First Minister of Scotland, and took the SNP from having just six out of fifty-nine seats in Scotland to winning fifty-six of them, leaving just three seats for the Tories, Labour and the Liberal Democrats to fight over. No other political party leader throughout history has achieved such a stunning result. You can see why *Forbes Magazine* voted her the second most powerful woman in the UK – second only to Her Majesty.

I ask the First Minister what the trick is to being so effective. Her answer is a modest deflection; she says she doesn't think she has any monopoly on that claim, but she will say this: *'Politics should not be seen as a career option. People who go into politics should be doing it because they are led by a deep sense of conviction. You need to have a sense of knowing why you're doing it and the people you're doing it for. And then you need to communicate that in a way that is relevant to their lives.'*

Nicola Sturgeon has that ability and then some. She is a brilliant communicator. Not in the sense of lofty phrases and soaring rhetoric, rather she manages to be both crystal clear and imbued with authentic passion whenever she speaks, while remaining calm and looking her audience right in the eye throughout. When she called the result of the EU referendum *'democratically unacceptable'* (Scotland had voted mainly to remain) in a tone of controlled and measured anger, no one was under any doubt as to what she meant and what she would want to do next. In even more plain-speaking terms, when some of the press suggested that the SNP's victory in the general election helped her arch-rivals the Tories into government, she summed up the claims as *'bollocks'*, a response entirely free of Scotch mist. In short, the First Minister of Scotland is a rare breed of politician: she says what she means and she *really* means what she says.

When I ask her what the conviction is that drives her, the First Minister eruditely sums it up in one word: *empowerment*. *'We are all better off if we are empowered to take more control over our own destiny. Obviously, that relates to Scotland as a country and the right to make our own decisions, but it relates to us as individuals and communities too. We should all be more empowered to shape the world around us.'*

This principle of self-determination at every level was seared into her at an early age. *'I grew up in the era of Margaret Thatcher, when unemployment in Scotland was sky-high, in a community decimated by deindustrialisation, which was caused by the political decisions of a government none of us had voted for. It was obvious to me that this was not right.'*

It was a female Labour MP coming into school and talking about her job that switched Nicola on to politics as a way to potentially tackle the social issues and injustices she saw around her. *'And I am very grateful to that lady for taking the time to talk to us that day, but there was an assumption that if you were going to go into politics in Scotland you would join the Labour Party, and I rebelled against that and found my home in the SNP.'* A decision entirely good for the SNP, and entirely disastrous for Labour.

Whether, long term, Nicola Sturgeon will achieve her lifelong wish and the founding aim of her party, independence for Scotland, remains to be seen. But there is no person more committed to, and better equipped for, the fight. Whatever your political views, she is a person who garners respect across the board, for the skills she deploys, the energy she sustains and, most of all, for the courage and consistency of her convictions. She is a woman who follows her own advice.

'STAND UP FOR WHAT YOU
BELIEVE IN. ALWAYS WITH
CONVICTION, WITH PASSION
AND INTEGRITY. DON'T
LET IDEOLOGY BLIND YOU,
BUT REMAIN TRUE TO
WHAT GUIDES YOU.

AND SPEAK IN YOUR OWN
VOICE, IN YOUR OWN WORDS,
IN A WAY THAT MAKES
SENSE TO YOU AND THAT
COULD NOT BE FROM
ANYONE ELSE.'

— *Nicola Sturgeon*

MUCHAS GRACIAS

WRITING HAS THE REPUTATION OF being a solitary endeavour, but this book was pure team sport.

The biggest thanks go to Head Coach and publisher Jamie Bada Byng, a man with enough energy to power all of West London and who most of the time seems to be actually doing so. He is the first and last word in passion, insight and encouragement, a door opener without equal and the man to call if you ever want chicken wings for breakfast.

My soothsaying agent Tony Topping was a consistent source of erudite advice and wise counsel. And was plain speaking enough to remind me of the basics of writing a book, not least that I would have to actually write it.

A big thank you to Sophie Sutcliffe, who, while heavily preggers, worked the phone lines and the inboxes and got us some great participants. And thanks to little Poppy for allowing her mum to do so.

Francesca Zampi, my erstwhile partner in crime and fellow hustler, was super encouraging from the get-go and opened her address book to me. Likewise Kim Chappell, who was an absolute tour de force of contacts, good vibes and emails, and a lovely person to drink tea with. Lucy McIntyre was a star in every sense and opened up New York, and Lizzie Ball, Nick Clegg and Alain de Botton were super kind and helpful in getting me in front of people as remarkable as themselves.

The team at Canongate have been an unfailingly professional, fun and smart group of people to work with and have made all of it a pleasure, with special thanks to Jo Dingley, who patiently guided the ship and kept it all together, Rafi Romaya for her artistic eye, Anna Frame and Jenny Fry for the fame generation, Lara Gardellini for the support and Jenny Todd for coming in and sorting it all out just when we needed it most.

Sam Kerr, as you will have seen with your own eyes, is a brilliant artist whose portraits have totally been the making of the book.

Behind the scenes there have been some people I may never meet but remain forever grateful to: the transcribers, especially our number one, Callum Crowe, and the delightful open-all-hours Debs Warner as copy editor in chief.

I am, of course, super grateful to each participant who lent their time, story and, most importantly, advice to the project.

And in terms of the gushy bits, an unconditional thank you to my mum and dad who to this day and, despite the many remarkably wise people I have met, continue to be the source of the best advice I have ever had, and to Nadia and Bay Rose, the result of listening to that advice and the people I have been waiting my whole life to meet.

THE CHARITIES

I'M LUCKY ENOUGH TO HAVE been on the receiving end of great advice and encouragement from my family, friends and role models, especially during my younger years when I didn't know any better. I realise not everyone is as fortunate. That is why all the author's profits from this book are going to be divided between the five mentoring and social inclusion charities below. They each do great work helping people who, for whatever reason, may need a few words of encouragement, a second chance or someone to help them plan the way ahead.

The Baytree Centre

A South London-based charity that promotes social inclusion for inner city families through education and training programmes for women and girls.

www.baytreecentre.org

Chance UK

A UK national mentoring charity focusing on children aged five to nine, helping to grow a child's strengths, build their self-esteem, and find positive alternatives to their challenging behaviour that could otherwise result in antisocial or criminal offending in later life.

www.chanceuk.com

Trailblazers UK

A charity based throughout the UK focused on young ex-offenders, that works to match up young people with trained volunteers and work with them to help turn their lives around so they can get on the right track and fit back into the community.

www.trailblazersmentoring.org.uk

Reach Out

A mentoring charity, based in London and Manchester, focusing on young people with behavioural issues, learning difficulties or confidence issues, supporting them to raise academic attainment and develop their character, by providing mentoring on a one-to-one basis from inspirational role models.

www.reachoutuk.org

St Giles Trust

A social inclusion charity with some gang-focused programmes, working to break the cycle of offending. They also support all kinds of disadvantaged people, from children through to adults, throughout the UK.

www.stgilestrust.org.uk

INDEX

BEHIND THE BOOK

Richard Reed studied geography at St. John's College, Cambridge before starting a career in advertising. A few years later he and two friends left their jobs to found Innocent Drinks. Starting from a market stall, today Innocent produces more than a million smoothies a day and sells them in seventeen countries across Europe. Reed is the founder of Art Everywhere and co-founder of the Innocent Foundation and JamJar Investments. He also presented the BBC Three series Be Your Own Boss. This is his first book.

Samuel Kerr employs a nomadic approach to his work, moving from process to process to find fresh ways to communicate ideas. His work spans portraiture, print design, art direction and brand identities, appearing across editorial, fashion, and food and drink industries. Embodying the nomadic approach, Samuel produced the portraits for this book on the road, during a tour of the UK.

www.samuelkerr.co.uk